THE
HOME DESIGN
HANDBOOK

THE HOME DESIGN HANDBOOK

THE ESSENTIAL PLANNING GUIDE FOR BUILDING, BUYING, OR REMODELING A HOME

JUNE COTNER MYRVANG
AND STEVE MYRVANG, A.I.A.

ILLUSTRATIONS BY JERRY JAMESON, B.AR.

AN OWL BOOK · HENRY HOLT AND COMPANY · NEW YORK

Published by Henry Holt and Company, Inc., 115 West 18th Street, New York, New York 10011.
Published in Canada by Fitzhenry & Whiteside Limited, 91 Granton Drive, Richmond Hill, Ontario L4B 2N5.

Library of Congress Cataloging-in-Publication Data
Myrvang, June Cotner.
The home design handbook : the essential planning guide for building, buying, or remodeling a home / June Cotner Myrvang and Steve Myrvang.—1st ed.
p.   cm.
''An Owl book.''
Includes bibliographical references.
1. Dwellings—Planning—Handbooks, manuals, etc.   2. Dwellings—Remodeling—Handbooks, manuals, etc.   3. Dwellings—Purchasing—Handbooks, manuals, etc.   I. Myrvang, Steve.   II. Title.
NA7115.M97   1992
728—dc20

91-28114
CIP

ISBN 0-8050-1833-6

Henry Holt books are available at special discounts for bulk purchases for sales promotions, premiums, fund-raising, or educational use. Special editions or book excerpts can also be created to specification. For details contact: Special Sales Director, Henry Holt and Company, Inc., 115 West 18th Street, New York, New York 10011.

First Edition—1992

DESIGNED BY LUCY ALBANESE

Printed in the United States of America
Recognizing the importance of preserving the written word, Henry Holt and Company, Inc., by policy, prints all of its first editions on acid-free paper.∞

10 9 8 7 6 5 4 3 2

To our clients and friends—
who offered ideas
and encouragement.

To our children,
Kyle and Kirsten—
who washed more than
their share of dishes.

CONTENTS

ACKNOWLEDGMENTS

We'd like to thank the following friends and professional acquaintances for their suggestions: Jerry Darnall, Steve Greenleaf, Susan Jenkins, Dean and Velma Johnson, Susan Lyons, Marianne Macdonald, Rick Nordquist, Ron Sharp, Ann and Austin Shotwell, Joyce Standish, William D. Tench, M.D., Christina S. Volkmann, John Wohlhaupter, and Lee Wunce.

The following architects helped us shape the book in its earliest phases: Bob Brown, Henry Osterman, and Charles B. Stephenson.

And in the final version, these three architects provided invaluable critique: Linda Berry Beal, Mary Staikos, A.I.A., and Peter Stoner, A.I.A.

Much appreciation goes to Denise Marcil, our literary agent, for seeing the possibilities in our earliest manuscript. Denise offered excellent suggestions and encouragement to help shape the book into its present form.

Our editor, Jo Ann Haun, made the process of turning a manuscript into a book as painless as possible. We were pleased to see the care that our manuscript received under her excellent guidance and to work with an editor who shared our excitement for the book.

A LETTER TO THE READER

Dear Reader,

Building or buying a home is the single greatest investment most people will ever make. For such a great expenditure, the home selected and its design ought to truly reflect the owner's needs, desires, and lifestyle. Too often though, money, energy, and time are spent in the pursuit or construction of a home and only later is it discovered that the home lacks qualities important to the homeowner. Most people feel uncomfortable wearing ill-fitting clothes, yet many live in untailored, off-the-rack homes designed for the "average" family. Perhaps the kitchen in an older home is too isolated for the new owner's "sit around the kitchen" entertaining style. Or maybe the bedrooms are too close to the family area, making a quiet bedtime difficult for early retirers.

Small, annoying problems are often not noticed until after the owners move in. Then, as they begin to use the spaces, they may recognize inadequate storage, too little counter space, too few electrical outlets in critical areas, and so on. These and many other commonsense features are often overlooked through a basic lack of planning. *The Home Design*

Handbook covers the specifics you need to consider before building, buying, or renovating your home, before a single dollar is spent in construction. And, perhaps more important, it will help you pin down the intangible qualities that make a house uniquely your home.

A few years ago, we designed a new home for ourselves, our children, and our animals. Even though we were professionals in the design field, we searched for a handbook or checklist to help us make sure our new home would suit our needs perfectly, but we could find nothing that really worked. What we did find, however, were the sometimes overwhelming details that kept appearing in designing our home. We discovered a way to organize these details simply and logically; the result is this book.

Our team effort worked well. My husband is a registered architect with twenty years of residential and commercial design experience. We have collaborated on many design projects. As a nonarchitect, I am often able to see design problems from a client's perspective, and have tried to write the book from this point of view, in nontechnical, accessible language.

We used earlier versions of this handbook with our residential clients with great success and continued to refine and develop the book's usefulness over a ten-year period. Clients often tell us that the handbook raises questions they had not thought to ask themselves. We find it opens a means of communication where no question is unimportant and helps save our clients, and us, from operating on different assumptions, reducing oversights and costly revisions.

The Home Design Handbook provides a structure in which to bring together the hopes, needs, and expectations of anyone planning to build, buy, or remodel a home, especially an environmentally responsible and energy-efficient home for the 1990s. For those contemplating buying an existing home, the handbook serves as an extensive checklist for evaluating both site and house. Those remodeling or building from the ground up will find that the handbook will help them avoid expensive and unforeseen changes once building is under way. In addition, architects, contractors, and home designers will find the handbook an invaluable resource in incorporating their clients' desires and ideas into the design before a single plan is drawn, and thus disagreements and misconceptions will be kept to a minimum.

Since many of our clients believe the design of their homes ought to be environmentally sound, we have included many energy-efficient ideas that will not add to the cost of construction. For example, the chapter on energy considerations shows how to maximize solar gain and minimize storm wind buffeting. The chapters on kitchen and living spaces explain ways to make recycling convenient and economize space and resources. Attention to detail at the planning stage results in the conservation of natural resources without additional cost.

Every site, individual, and project budget is different. *The Home Design Handbook* provides complete checklists and exercises designed to assist individuals in developing an understanding of what they really want in a home.

We will appreciate your comments and suggestions. Address your letters to:

Myrvang Architects
19351 8th Avenue N.E.
Poulsbo, Washington 98370
(206) 697-9434

June Cotner Myrvang
Steve Myrvang, A.I.A.

HOW TO USE
THIS HANDBOOK

Whether you are remodeling a room or building a new home from scratch, *The Home Design Handbook* will help you create the home of your dreams. If you intend to remodel only one room or area, complete Chapters 1, 3, 4, 16, and particularly Chapter 5 ("For the Remodeler"). Then go directly to the chapter that pertains to your particular project, such as kitchens. However, if you are not certain about the extent of your remodeling needs or if you wonder whether a certain existing home or specific house plan will fit your needs, then work through the entire book as if you were building a new home. Your responses to the questions will help you decide which features fit your needs and suit your family's lifestyle.

Designing and building a home involves an enormous number of decisions. This book will help clarify the needs of everyone in the household. If this is a shared family project, it makes sense to resolve conflicts before detailed plans are drawn. Every hour spent in planning could well save you three hours at the construction site. After everyone has responded to the exercises in this book, sort through your differences to decide upon some satisfying compromises before you meet with your design professional. Trade-offs are inevitable. It is often necessary to sacrifice one idea to accomodate another—or to meet your budget.

Make sure, too, that your vision is a practical one for your current lifestyle. For example, if you're ready to retire and travel, you'll likely want a home that requires low maintenance and is easy to close up and leave, certainly not the palace you dreamed about in your twenties and thirties. If your family is young, you'll want a home that is easy to pay for and finished with materials that can withstand plenty of action.

Some design considerations are standard; we have included a "Checklist" section, where needed, for these key items. *Make sure your design professional is aware of every checklist, because it is not unusual for simple considerations to be overlooked.* The checklist appears before each section requiring your individual responses, so you will not need to duplicate this information in your responses. Some chapters offer narratives: explanations of important, yet often unfamiliar, home design information.

We encourage you to keep a notebook of photographs illustrating your favorite architectural elements, spaces, and specific finish details, such as window styles, a particular kitchen sink, a specific lighting fixture, and appealing paint combinations. When you meet with your design professional you will be better prepared to communicate what visually and programmatically appeals to you.

Also, read some of the excellent books listed in the Annotated Bibliography at the end of this book. We purposefully chose to provide primary information in our book, knowing that interested readers could seek more detailed explanations in other sources.

Enjoy the handbook! Here is the opportunity to make your home uniquely suited to your lifestyle, tastes, and budget. Build a fire. Put on your favorite music. Let's get started.

THE
HOME DESIGN
HANDBOOK

· ·

HOME IS WHERE YOUR HEART CAN LIVE

"Making a house work for you, getting it to deliver the emotional rewards—love, personal expression, and a sense of well-being— requires knowing yourself and knowing how you'd like to live. Your house is that special place where you can be you."

—JoAnn Barwick,
House Beautiful

CHECKLIST

(No response is required. These are standard items that should not be overlooked.)

1. Does the home complement the natural surroundings and existing neighborhood?

2. Are undesirable sights and sounds screened out by location of walls, windows, and entries?

3. Does natural light enter from two sides of every room? (See pages 7, 8, and 11.)

4. Is there natural light in the hallway?

5. Is there cross-ventilation in each habitable space? (Rooms should have two outside walls with windows to accomplish this.)

6. Is the house designed for privacy from the street and from the neighbors? (Would you feel comfortable walking around in a bathrobe through all parts of the house?)

WHAT FEELS LIKE HOME

Where do we find emotional value, the qualities of the heart we want most in our homes? How can we incorporate these qualities into our home design?

Childhood memories often contain vivid images that trigger deeply held feelings of love, joy, and peacefulness. As young people, we were more receptive to the simple pleasures that we are often too busy to enjoy as adults. Perhaps you had an aunt who fed you peach pie à la mode inside a sunlit screened porch. Or maybe your first home had a window seat just big enough for you and all your dolls or toy soldiers. Was your kitchen table close enough to your mother at the stove so that you could hear her softly humming over the crackling bacon? Did you ever climb into a tree house bathed in dappled light breaking through green maple leaves?

As children, we were not busy making money, keeping appointments, and meeting deadlines. Memories of our youth may recall places we could enjoy simply being in. Bringing these memories to the creative design process may assist in making your house feel like home, and represent for each of us places of the heart.

The following exercises are designed to stimulate your thoughts on what feels like home. Your answers about design goals you have recently formed and your heartfelt memories will assist you and your design professional in creating a space that feels right for you and the way you live.

What can be derived from these exercises is the recognition of qualities or details that have always invoked warm feelings. Your house design can be relevant to your family's present lifestyle and still provide the continuity of rich feelings that you would find in an old friend or a warm memory.

Ask yourself questions such as: What impact does light (natural or artificial) have on this image? How do I feel about the finishes? Are they warm, soft, and inviting, or crisp, cool, and stylish? What about the size of the space (or building)? Is it stretched horizontally or vertically? What are the relationships of the built portions of the image to the natural environment? Does it fit in or stand out? How is my personality encouraged by this image? Do I prefer to be alone in the scene or with a group of people?

It is best to approach the following exercises when you are relaxed and rested. We are confident that you will be filled with ideas and memories that can be successfully incorporated into your new home. While the questions are purposely brief, your answers need not be. Write freely; don't judge or edit what comes forward. There are no wrong ideas in creative design.

EXERCISE 1: GENERAL FEELINGS

1. What feeling do you want to have as you drive or walk up to your home? Be specific.

2. What is most important to you in a home?

3. From other homes you have been in, what have you seen that most appeals to you?

4. How many years do you plan to live in your home?

5. Pleasant memories of childhood spaces are helpful to your designer. Think back to your favorite indoor childhood spaces. Which rooms of your previous homes are most memorable?

6. Why did you enjoy those rooms?

7. How did those rooms make you feel?

8. What houses of friends and relatives did you enjoy visiting?

   Why?

9. What vacation homes did you enjoy visiting?

Why?

Located on top of a knoll, this contemporary farmhouse was designed to allow natural light to enter from two sides of every room and for efficient heating and ventilation, all on a limited budget. The design criteria were achieved, as (1) natural light streams into all living and bedroom spaces—in addition, all four bedrooms receive desired eastern morning sunlight; (2) the kitchen, dining, and living areas receive warm southern sunlight; (3) an open design allows the entire home to be heated with a fan-operated high-efficiency fireplace; and (4) the home is well ventilated in summer because of window placements and a ventilating skylight.

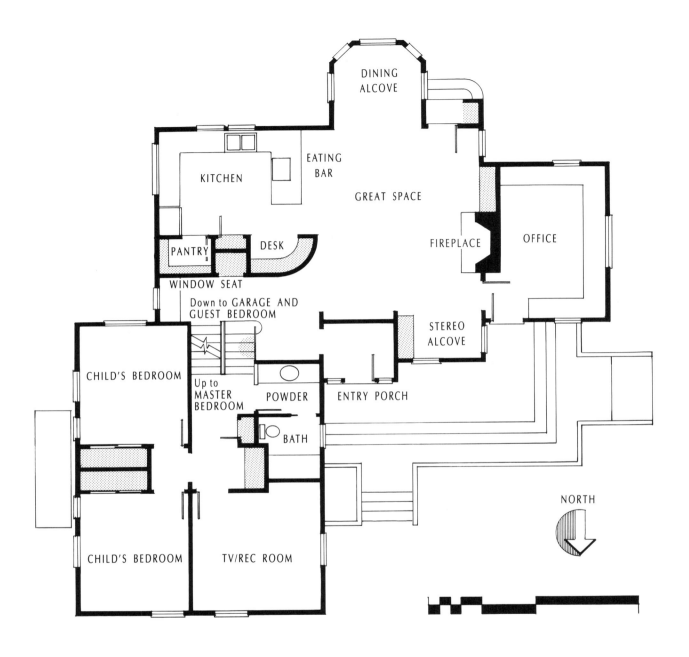

DINING
ALCOVE

KITCHEN

EATING
BAR

GREAT SPACE

FIREPLACE

OFFICE

PANTRY

DESK

WINDOW SEAT

Down to GARAGE AND
GUEST BEDROOM

STEREO
ALCOVE

CHILD'S BEDROOM

Up to
MASTER
BEDROOM

POWDER

ENTRY PORCH

BATH

NORTH

CHILD'S BEDROOM

TV/REC ROOM

This is a partial floor plan of the house on the previous page. The owners enjoy living informally, so the ''great space''
works well for small gatherings and large parties. The cooks can interact directly with those in the living area—and also
enjoy the warm flicker of the fireplace. The dining alcove is located next to the kitchen, for convenience, yet the kitchen
counters are not visible to diners. The bucolic scene of the children riding their horses in the pasture can be viewed from
the south-facing kitchen, dining, and living spaces. Shaded areas indicate storage for each living space.

10. Do you prefer living spaces that

    —— flow together?

    —— have separate formal and informal areas?

    —— open visually to a garden or a view?

11. Do you prefer to have most of the floor space in your home divided into individual rooms that can be closed off?

    If so, which spaces should have an open plan?

12. Do you want to separate any areas from visitors? (You should consider how tidy you generally keep your home and what you do and do not want your drop-in guests to see.)

13. Do you often have different activities happening at once that might benefit from acoustical separation, such as music practice, TV watching, homework, loud play?

Which rooms should be separated acoustically?

An interior photo of the "great space" illustration on page 8. Note how the 4'9"-high curved wall provides definition and separation for the kitchen area.

14. Often there are seasonal as well as weekly and daily differences in the way we use our homes. (You might spend rainy winter evenings cuddled by a fireplace, while on hot summer days you might want to be able to open the living room to the outdoors.) How do you envision this happening?

Does this suggest specific requirements in any rooms?

To help you decide on feelings and practical considerations for each room, complete the following two exercises. The first is very general, and the second will help you think about the function of each room.

EXERCISE 11: ROOMS AND QUALITIES DESIRED

List each room you want, ideally, in your home and the qualities desired. Use some of the following adjectives or make up your own:

light, spacious, dramatic
visual connection to outdoors
family gathering place
for children, noisy
cozy/comforting
formal/grand
quiet/intimate
efficient
playful
other:_____

Room or Area   *Qualities*

_____   _____

_____   _____

_____   _____

_____   _____

_____   _____

_____   _____

_____   _____

_____   _____

_____   _____

_____   _____

_____   _____

EXERCISE III: HOUSEHOLD ACTIVITIES

List each room again and add the function it will serve. See if you need to change any of the adjectives in Exercise II.

HOUSEHOLD ACTIVITIES

1. entertaining
2. relaxing
3. reading
4. listening to music
5. formal conversation
6. intimate conversation
7. child play (noisy)
8. playing games
9. watching TV
10. telephone conversations
11. food preparation
12. casual eating
13. dining
14. sleeping
15. daytime naps
16. bathing
17. dressing
18. laundering
19. desk work/bill paying
20. studying
21. meditation (quiet time)
22. hobbying
23. sewing
24. making music
25. playing loud music
26. exercising
27. storing

Room or Area

Functions/Activities

_____   _____

_____   _____

_____   _____

_____   _____

_____   _____

_____   _____

_____   _____

_____   _____

_____   _____

_____   _____

_____   _____

_____   _____

"With property values soaring and accommodation becoming more and more scarce, people everywhere are having to adjust to living in increasingly small spaces. Like all restrictions, however, this one can encourage great resourcefulness and creativity; it can focus attention on your needs and tastes and help you to recognize the potential of your rooms as well as their limitations. With imagination and careful planning, you can make every part of your home so comfortable and attractive that the reaction it inspires in visitors is not so much, 'What a clever use of space,' as 'What a lovely room.' "

—Lorrie Mack, "Taking Stock,"
Conran's Living in Small Spaces

2

SITE CONSIDERATIONS

"My prescription for a modern house: first, a good site. Pick one that has features making for character. Then build your house so that you may still look from where you stood upon all that charmed you and lose nothing of what you saw before the house was built, but see more."

—Frank Lloyd Wright

CHOOSING A BUILDING SITE: Soil, Water Flow, Solar Access, and More

When first stepping on a piece of land, how do you decide whether it's right for your home? What will be your practical and aesthetic considerations?

Most of us want pleasant views, sunlight, and privacy. Other considerations, though more subtle, may have a major impact on the relationship of house to site and should be carefully addressed in the site-planning stages. Issues such as soil stability and an environmentally sensitive location may require the hiring of a specialist to properly assess costs and impact. Other issues will require investigative work on your part: Where might future development occur? What are the plans for the large parcels of land contiguous to yours? How can privacy be maintained? This is especially important when buying for the peaceful solitude of country living.

Your choice of a building site will sometimes be limited by where the soil percolates, which indicates where you can place your septic drainfield. If a well is required, you will need to maintain adequate setbacks from any septic fields.

What if you find a too-good-to-be-true view lot on a steeply sloped hillside? Your added construction costs (excavation, foundations, retaining walls, drainage, and access) will need to be added to the too-good-to-be-true price. The financial repercussions are often underestimated unless construction costs are carefully analyzed. Before purchasing a "problem" site, make the offer contingent upon satisfactory investigation of these costs. Then hire an architect, a soils engineer, and perhaps a structural engineer to help you determine them.

Other too-good-to-be-true deals may be found in wetland properties. Perhaps the wonderful photo you clipped from *Country Home* of the cottage with the pond and lily pads pushed right up to the front porch may become a nightmare to make a reality. The approval process for building in an environmentally sensitive wetlands area could easily last over a year. If you build in the 1990s, a one-hundred-foot setback between the pond and house might be required to comply with wetlands regulations. Finally, boggy soils may require expensive wood or concrete piles set deep to rest on bearing soil.

On a larger parcel, you will need to obtain cost estimates for putting in a road to your building site. Observe surface water flow patterns during a heavy rainfall; your road may need culverts for proper drainage. Beware of rock outcroppings, which may require blasting to achieve desired finish grades.

When you have a choice about where to place your home, determine the effects of air temperature and convection on the site. Valley sites are often the recipients of cold air dropping down hillside slopes. Consider the effects of storm winds on your site. Trees located a safe distance from your house will likely provide welcome wind protection.

SITE FEATURES TO PRESERVE

With practical concerns satisfied, you can now look at your site from an aesthetic standpoint. Is the native vegetation attractive and hardy? If so, this may decrease your landscaping costs. Try to envision your property at different seasons before you build. What is the effect of a blanket of snow? Camp on your property in the spring or summer. Can you hear birds singing in the early morning? Can you hear the wind rustle through the leaves? Can you hear the gurgling of a nearby brook? Notice the play of light through trees in the early evening sun. Be respectful of your responses to these subtle matters. Enjoying nature in its simplest form is sometimes more important, and certainly less expensive, than a fantastic "view" site.

When you have decided on a piece of land and know approximately where you want to build on the site, fine-tune this location with potential solar access. Will the site allow for a long east-west axis home with a southern orientation?

Now look at subtle differences. Do you feel more a part of the land just below the hill's crest than on top? Are there naturally framed views? Often, such views will have a more pleasing impact than full views.

Take a tape measure, five-foot-long stakes, and string to your property; stake out the boundaries of a typical house. Visualize your home on the site. You have much freedom of choice at this point; simply move your string.

During the preliminary design of your home, you and your designer should take the plans to your site and stake out outside house-corner boundaries. Bring a transit or builder's level to determine typical floor elevations. If at all possible, climb a tall ladder and see what your view will be from different locations of your home. If you see something better, it's inexpensive to make changes at this stage, before your drawings are finalized.

Taking time to appreciate the subtle differences of your site will reward you in making the interaction of your home and site as pleasing to you as possible. Your care in site selection will foster reverence for the land that is entrusted to you and will extend the feelings and images of your home well beyond its outside walls.

TECHNICAL EXERCISES: ASSESSING A BUILDING SITE

The following are questions that should be answered before purchasing your land or before designing your house. Many of your answers may suggest legal consequences when you apply for your building permit.

1. Is there good year-round road access to your site? (If not, have you determined the cost of installing a road or upgrading an existing one?)

2. If you need to install a septic system, has your site passed a percolation test? (A percolation test determines the rate at which a particular soil absorbs effluent: A hole is dug in the soil and filled with water, then

the rate at which the water level drops is measured. In certain localities, perc tests can only be performed during specific times of year.)

How many bedrooms are allowed by the local building code with your septic system's capacity?

3. Are power, phone, cable TV, and water* available on your building site? (If not, have you determined the cost of these improvements?)

Is there a time delay for water or utility hookups?

4. If you wish to heat, cook, or start fires with natural gas, is it available on your building site?

*If you are not on city water, a well could be a costly expense. One never knows how far one will need to go for water until the well drilling ends. A new well can run anywhere from $3,000 to $12,000 (and perhaps more). For a rough cost approximation, approach neighboring property owners and find out the depth of their wells. You may wish to ask your neighbors about the possibility of upgrading their well to a two-family or a community well system. (If this option is viable, you would need to pay a fee to the well owner and all upgrade costs.)

5. Have you determined a logical place for your building site?

6. Does your building site have good natural drainage?

7. Has your property been surveyed?

   Is each boundary corner accurately marked?

8. Is your lot a legal building lot or must you create a new lot through a short plat? (Contact local planning authorities for more information regarding these processes.)

9. Are there any easements on your property? (An easement is a right-of-way granted to a person or company authorizing access to or over the owner's land. An electric company obtaining a right-of-way across private property is a common example. Granting ingress or

egress for a neighboring property is another. Building construction is usually prohibited in the easement area.)

10. What are the setbacks for your project? (Front, side, and rear setbacks are the minimum allowable distances from the house to the property lines. This information can usually be obtained from your local planning department.)

11. What is the maximum allowable height for your project? (This height is usually restricted and is generally measured from the average grade to the mid-height of the roof.)

12. Has any part of the land been filled?

13. Has a soils engineer inspected your building site to determine soil stability and soil-bearing capacity?

14. Will earth moving be involved?

15. Are any portions of your property steeply sloped?

16. Are there seasonal limitations restricting your building time?

17. What zoning ordinances apply to your property? (Zoning ordinances are acts of an authorized local government establishing building codes and setting forth regulations for property land usage.)

18. Are there restrictive covenants that could prohibit you from building what you want? (Restrictive covenants are private restrictions limiting the use of real property. Restrictive covenants are created by deed and may "run with the land," binding all subsequent purchasers of the land, or they may be "personal" and binding only between

the original seller and buyer. Restrictive covenants may limit the density of buildings per acre; regulate size, style, or price range of buildings to be erected; or prevent particular businesses from operating in a given area.)

19. Is there a local design review board that must approve your plans?

20. Are there bodies of water on your property, large or small? If so, describe. (They may be subject to wetlands regulations.)

21. Is there excessive ground water on your property that may require drainage lines or culverts?

22. Do shoreline regulations apply to your property?

23. Are you aware of any subsurface conditions that may affect your project, such as a high water table, springs, expansive soils, root systems of major trees, or frostline depth? (Talk with neighboring property owners and consult with a soils engineer if you suspect

your property may have some of these problems. Note: If your water table is high, a basement may be unfeasible.)

24. What is the allowable percentage of lot coverage for your project? (For example, many zoning codes allow for a maximum of 35 percent of the lot to be covered by a built structure.)

25. Have you located all existing underground utility lines, septic and fuel tanks, abandoned wells, and/or any other subsurface structures that may affect building location and foundations? (For locating utility lines, contact your local utility company. Your best bet for obtaining information on any subsurface structures would be from previous property owners. Unfortunately, the way these structures are usually discovered is: Oops!)

26. Will your project interfere with your neighbors' views or solar access? (See opposite page.)

Can this be avoided?

27. Is your project's solar access and view protected from future development and/or maturing trees? (See above.)

Neighboring tall structures throw a long shadow.

28. Is your building site above depressions where cool air collects?

29. Are you in an area of frequent or extended power outages?

    Will you require a generator for backup sources of heat or power?

30. Are electrical storms an occasional problem in your area? (If so, an electrician should install a surge protector on your fuse box.)

Are electrical storms a frequent problem in your area? (If so, you should have the protection of a professionally installed grounding system.)

31. Are there any other hazards in your area such as earthquakes, floods, landslides, or danger of fire?

32. How close is the nearest fire station? (Call your homeowner's insurance carrier to confirm that the distance is acceptable for fire insurance coverage. If not, you may want to install a fire sprinkler system. See Table 1, page 215, for a discussion of these systems.)

33. What is the direction of prevailing winds?

Summer _____   Winter _____

Will your site have protection from winter winds?

Do summer breezes cool your site?

34. Are you aware of any construction problems your lot may present?

Outside wall connects the house and garage, creating a windbreak and entry court.

35. Are there special trees, plants, or features that you want to protect during construction? (In a remodel, you will also want to protect septic fields, walks, and decks.)

36. What time period is required to obtain a building permit in your area?

What are the fees?

AESTHETIC EXERCISES: FINE-TUNING

1. What do you like most about your site?

2. What site features are you interested in preserving or featuring?

3. Is privacy, or the lack of it, a consideration for your lot? If so, describe.

Does your site require special screening to ensure visual or auditory privacy?

4. What are your thoughts about sun location and view potential for your site? (For example, in warm climates, southwest exposure should be avoided. Late afternoon sun is much hotter than eastern morning sun. In cold climates, a sunny southwest exposure is often desirable, especially if there are deciduous trees that diffuse the sun in summer and allow it in during the winter. Refer to the illustration on page 32 for a more detailed explanation.)

In the heating climate, provide your home with good winter sun access from the south. In the summer, shade your home with deciduous trees, generous overhangs, or window coverings to prevent excessive solar heat buildup. Insulation is a key element in making your home energy efficient.

The transition climate benefits from solar backup of winter heating as well as careful shading in the summer. Air-conditioning demands may be lessened with proper orientation and ventilation, allowing cool summer breezes to pass through the home.

The cooling climate requires insulation to protect the inside from the hot, uncomfortable outside, except in the Southeast, where natural air circulation is essential to lessen the impact of high humidity. Midday shading of outside spaces with roofs, trellises, or overhangs provides greater outdoor comfort and encourages people outside, lessening air-conditioning demands.

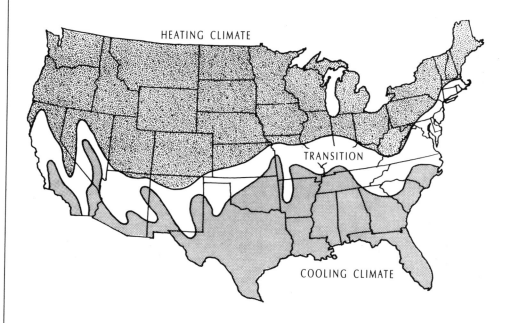

5. If you have room for only one large yard, do you prefer it in the front or in the back of the house?

6. What site activities or functions will you require room for? (Examples: play yard, lap pool, gardening, and so forth.)

"Children enjoy both 'defined play' on objects like swings and slides, which have been designed for specific uses, and 'creative play' in areas such as sandboxes where they use their imaginations to build castles, villages, roads, rivers, and bridges. A space that is designed to accommodate both types of play will stimulate children physically and mentally for hours."

—Elizabeth Murray and Derek Fell, "Children's Play Spaces,"
Home Landscaping

3

ENERGY CONSIDERATIONS

"Now in houses with a south aspect, the sun's rays penetrate into the porticoes in winter, but in summer the path of the sun is right over our heads and above the roof, so that there is shade. If, then, this is the best arrangement, we should build the south side loftier to get the winter sun and the north side lower to keep out the cold winds."

—Socrates, as quoted by
Xenophone in Memorabilia

ENERGY EFFICIENCY IN DESIGN

Ninety percent of the energy we use comes from nuclear power or fossil fuels, both of which generate toxic wastes. Also, fossil fuel supplies are rapidly diminishing, rising in cost, and most recently, contributing to global warming. A key to promoting a healthy environment is to find ways to use less energy. Energy efficiency can best be achieved by carefully evaluating heat generation, heat transfer, heat loss, and heat storage. It costs only one-tenth as much to save energy through conservation measures as it does to produce more energy. A home's initial design can contribute significantly to reduced energy consumption.

THINK SMALL

This is the first rule of energy efficiency. The smaller your home, the less energy is needed to heat and light it, and less energy will have been used to build it. By downscaling one's needs, a small home or cottage may be the answer to affordability. Also, less space to maintain provides a simpler lifestyle. Ask yourself if two spaces can be combined to reduce square footage. For example, incorporating the kitchen into the living area, creating a "great space," has the added benefit of a less-confined space for preparing meals and lends a more open feeling to a smaller living area. Small homes, however, present their own design challenges, including the need for special attention to storage needs (see Chapter 12, "Storage Areas and Closets").

EFFICIENT SHAPES

Energy conservation studies show that the most efficient buildings enclose as much space as possible with the least amount of wall and roof exposed to the weather. Homes lose a great deal of heat through the roof. Thus, a two- or three-story home is generally more energy-efficient than a one-story design. It makes more sense to increase size by adding a second or third floor than it does to expand the floor plan. Also, multistory homes have lower foundation costs.

Multistory homes generally are easier to heat and cool because use can be made of convection currents within the home for distribution of air. Rooms on the top floor will be the warmest. In an area of hot summers, first-floor bedrooms may be more comfortable. In cold climates, one might want to locate bedrooms on upper floors, for added warmth.

LOCATION, SITING, AND ORIENTATION

The placement of your home in relation to the sun, wind, and trees can significantly reduce energy consumption. In most of the country you will be looking for protection from chilling winter winds and for exposure to summer breezes. Working with nature is the fundamental principle. In the southeastern United States, locating the house to take advantage of natural breezes may assist in reducing dehumidification needs. In moderate to cold climates, the main window area of a home should face south so

In cold and moderate climates, siting a home to receive protection from winter winds will make it more energy-conserving. In North America, prevailing winds blow from west to east, but seasonal and regional exceptions exist, such as warm, moist breezes from the south, and cold, dry winds from the north.

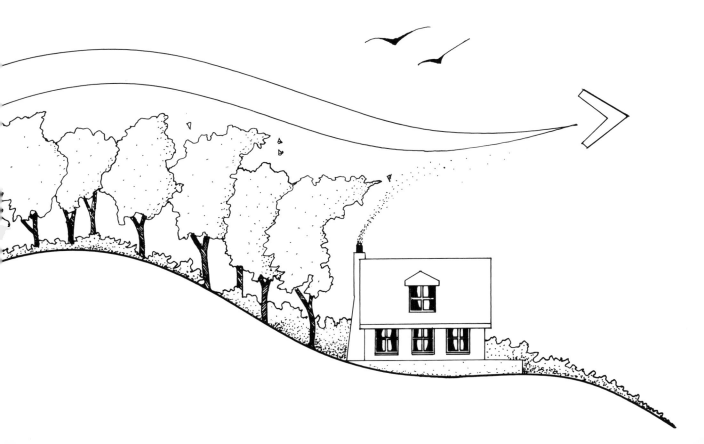

solar heat can be collected through your windows. The north side of your home should have minimal windows. Garages or other unheated storage spaces may be located on the north side to create an insulating sheath. In warm climates, the opposite may be true: A garage on the south or west can block unwanted heat from the summer sun.

Four simple rules describe how different exposures will affect your home: North-facing slopes are cold, receiving little sun; south-facing slopes are warm; slopes that face east will be warm in the morning, but will not receive direct sunlight in the late afternoon; and west-facing slopes may be cool all morning, then overheat in the afternoon. Given a choice, building on a slope facing south makes the best sense for homes in moderate to cold climates. For example, locating a house on a twenty-degree south slope provides nearly an equivalent solar gain to moving your house to flat ground 1,360 miles to the south.

Both water and ice reflect solar radiation at low winter sun angles. The drawing opposite shows the benefit of placing a house north of a body of water. Measurements show an increase of up to 65 percent in solar radiation received through south-facing windows due to solar reflection.

The location, siting, and orientation of a home can all contribute to maximizing the warmth of the winter sun and optimizing any shelter given by hills and trees against prevailing winter winds. A well-sited home will use the natural features of the locale to maximize energy efficiency and, therefore, will never have to draw as much supplementary energy as one built without any regard for its surroundings. The importance of spending time on your site to experience both its positive and negative qualities cannot be overstated.

INSULATION AND BLOCKING AIR INFILTRATION

If your budget for improving your home's energy efficiency is limited, your best investment will be in insulation and weatherproofing to protect against air infiltration (cold air seeping in through cracks and pushing lighter, heated air out). No other factors mentioned in this chapter will have a more profound impact than insulation and weatherproofing on reducing energy consumption. According to the U.S. Department of

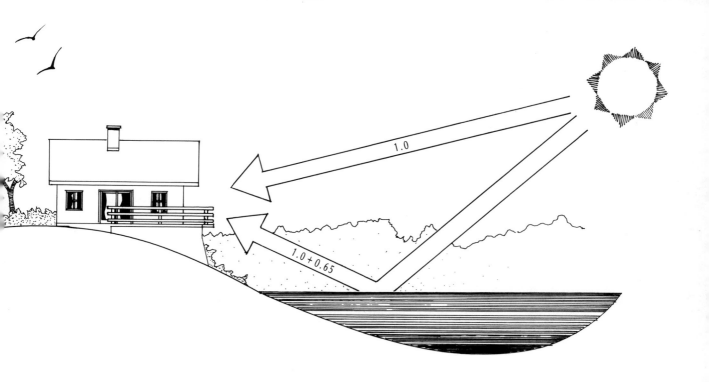

Placing the house north of a body of water increases the solar radiation by 65 percent through south-facing windows.

Energy, "50 percent to 70 percent of the energy used in the average American home is for heating and cooling." Many energy-saving building materials are available: expandable sealants, window films that hold heat inside the house or keep it outside, and plastic membranes that control moisture transmission and air infiltration.

The infiltration/vapor barrier is important in all climates and critical in ones with freezing temperatures. The vapor barrier is applied along the inside of studs, ceiling joists, and floor joists to prevent the movement of moisture from the living areas into the insulation, which loses some of its efficiency when it becomes damp. In humid climates, where air-conditioning removes moisture from the inside air, the vapor barrier will prevent outside moisture from entering the living areas.

Since 1980, superinsulated homes have grown in popularity. Insulation quality is expressed in R values, which reflect the ability of a material to resist the passage of heat. While many well-insulated homes have R values of R-19 in the walls and R-38 in the roof, superinsulated homes can have R-60 insulation values in both the walls and ceilings. Superinsulated homes retain heat so well that proponents often talk about capturing the heat given off by occupants, appliances, and household lighting. While superinsulation is best suited to colder climates, it is also an effective barrier against incoming heat in warm climates.

Three main types of insulating materials are available: Batts, blown-in, and rigid. Batts insulation is the most common, but care must be taken to fill all corners. Choose a higher-priced material that will not degrade with moisture. Blown-in insulation allows for maximal insulation in large attic cavities. A common installation would use batts in exterior walls and blown-in insulation in the attic. Rigid insulation is the most costly but requires less thickness and can be placed against soil and moisture without degrading. It is most often used against foundation walls or under floor slabs.

A recently developed insulation system, Blown-in Batts System (BIBS), provides higher insulation values than batts insulation in walls and roof cavities. With BIBS, a netting is attached to the inside of the framing. The insulating material, in the form of a glue fog, is blown into the cavities, filling all small cracks. When dry, the glue prevents the insulation from settling.

Although preventing air leakage (infiltration) with caulking and weatherstripping will reduce heat loss, it is essential that adequate fresh air is introduced into the home. Fresh air exchange will be discussed later in this chapter.

LANDSCAPING

Deciduous trees and arbors (see the illustration on page 44) placed on the south and west sides of the house offer shade protection in the summer. The average mature tree cools the air around its base eight to ten degrees during the summer months; that is the equivalent of twenty room-sized air conditioners working ten hours a day. When the leaves drop in the fall, the sun can enter south-facing windows and warm the house. In selecting a shade tree, find out when the tree gains and drops its leaves for your particular climate.

Evergreen trees may act as windbreaks, lessening wind chill on cool, breezy days.

CONSERVATION

Energy conservation is important because 36 percent of the energy consumed in the United States is used to heat, cool, ventilate, and light buildings, and run appliances such as refrigerators, television sets, and computers. Any time you can light your home without flipping a switch, you save energy.

Skylights and clerestories are one such route to free lighting, but their use must be balanced by increased heat loss. Skylights are built in the roof, while clerestories are windows that fit in walls near the ceiling; both are positioned high to gather the light that comes from above. In planning your home, put your light gatherers where they will provide daytime light such as in your kitchen and work areas. A skylight not only lets in the sunshine, it visually opens the room, making it appear more spacious. Skylights and clerestories should be double- or triple-glazed to minimize heat loss.

Windows are a trade-off; they provide views and natural lighting but also create problems for heating and cooling. Also, some individuals feel uncomfortable at night with huge expanses of glass; they feel that they're being watched from the outside. Most people with a great view want to enjoy it and are willing to accept some heat loss or heat gain. Use window products that allow light transmission while providing insulation.

Before the advent of air-conditioning, people cooled their homes by opening windows and vents, thereby creating air movement. These techniques still work. A single open-screened skylight placed at the top of open stairs can vent several volumes of house air per hour, inducing a breeze through open downstairs windows and doors at the same time. Also, ceiling fans have become popular, creating breezes that make hot, humid weather more tolerable. Usually, undesirable summer solar heat gain occurs not at midday, when the sun beats on the roof, but at mid-morning from the east and at mid-afternoon from the west. If you are serious about not having an air conditioner, you must shade not only south but east and west windows as well during those times.

Remember, the most cost-effective place to put your energy dollars is in insulation, which keeps heat in during the cold and keeps the house cool when it's warm outside. Also, weatherproofing your home costs far less than installing solar panels. To immediately save energy in colder climates, weatherstrip your doors and windows and insulate the attic and hot water tank. (For more ideas, refer to Table 2, "Energy Conservation Measures," pages 216–17.)

NATURAL HEAT GENERATION

The following heat-generating systems are ecologically sound. They have no harmful by-products and generate energy using natural sources. The transition from fossil fuels to renewable power sources has never been more justified than in this age of environmental pollution, limited energy resources, and worldwide population increase.

SOLAR POWER

Due to the inexhaustible abundance of sunlight, direct conversion of solar energy may well be the cornerstone of a sustainable world energy system. Locating windows, skylights, and glass doors on the south side of the house is a basic way to maximize solar gain. Care must be taken, however, to provide shading from direct southern sunlight in the summer or excessive energy may be expended on air-conditioning.

The best solar designs conserve energy while making the most of the sun's warmth. Solar methods of heating the home can be categorized as either passive (dependent on home construction) or active (dependent upon mechanical devices). With a passive solar system, heat is generated when sunlight strikes interior surfaces after passing through glass. A well-insulated building with curtains or thermal shutters over the windows retains the heat. Often, natural thermal movement—convection, conduction, and radiation—is all that is needed to circulate the heat. Popular cathedral ceilings are summertime bonuses because they allow warm air to rise well above head level; the air can then be vented out of a rooftop ridge vent or an open skylight. In winter, a quiet-operating ceiling fan

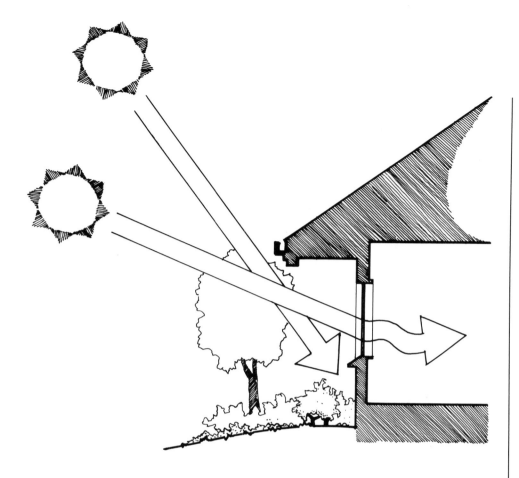

The low path of the sun during winter provides direct sunlight and warmth through south-facing windows. Summer heat gain is prevented by extending the roof over vertical windows. Note: Overhangs greater than two feet will cause unwanted shading during spring months in many climates.

or a furnace's summer fan may be used to circulate warm air back down to the room's occupants. It is important that the amount of passive solar glazing is balanced with adequate thermal storage mass (described later) and a proper distribution system, which should be designed by a professional.

Adequate shading is vital during the summer months in hot climates. Many people use overhangs or trellises on south-, west-, and sometimes east-facing windows. (See pages 43 and 44.) Exterior shades are preferable to interior shades because interior shades permit the sun to heat the window glass, therefore the heat has already come inside the home. For east and west windows, in the early morning, the sun is too low to block completely with an overhang. In the late afternoon, you will need deciduous trees or indoor sunscreens such as blinds, insulating panels, curtains, or shades for these windows.

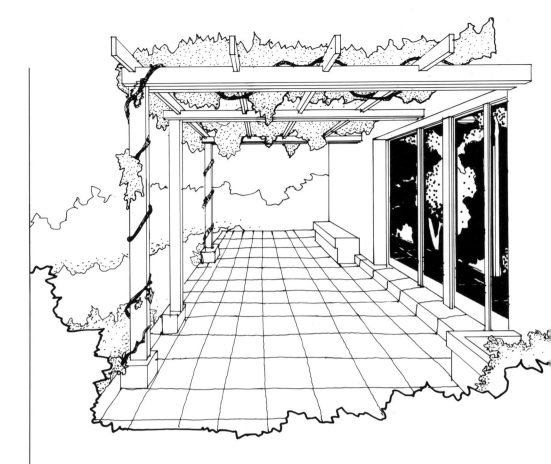

A vine-laden trellis provides shade and a cozy outside space.

For those living in southern climates, if glass is installed in a location with direct solar access, make sure the glass has a shade coefficient (a heat protection number). Shade coefficient windows are shaded like sunglasses; the outside view will be darker, yet heat accumulation will be reduced.

An active solar system requires mechanical components such as solar panels, which absorb the sun's heat and may store it in water tanks or rock beds. Pumps and ducts are required to circulate the heat with the aid of fans, valves, and thermostats. Although long praised as alternatives to fossil fuels, active solar heating systems are often costly and undependable.

Passive solar systems, however, require little or no maintenance since there are no mechanical parts. The initial installation and maintenance costs are low, so they repay the investment in a short period of time. If you are building a new home, basic solar heating can be incorporated at virtually no additional cost because passive solar systems employ careful placement of conventional materials already required, such as glass and concrete. A passive solar system is most often used as an efficient supplement to a conventional heating system.

Passive solar homes often have a long east-west axis so the broad sides of the home can face south and north. North-facing windows are few and small to reduce heat loss. Many passive solar homes have greenhouses that gather heat and also provide cheerful, sunny places to sit.

Passive solar homes do require active participation if the energy benefits are to be fully realized. Fans need to be turned on, doors opened, vents and insulating blinds adjusted. Many people find that passive solar homes offer a sense of well-being. They appreciate the attractive building materials and the added interior sunlight, which creates sunny nooks for reading, writing, and sewing.

Solar effectiveness varies with climate. Ideal locations are where winters are clear, sunny, and cold. Standard weather statistics, which usually include heating degree-days and percent cloud cover, are useful in determining solar applicability.

For additional solar calculations and alternative energy information, refer to the books listed in the Annotated Bibliography. Also, contact your local state energy extension service (Table 3) and the national solar organizations (Table 4).

PHOTOVOLTAIC POWER

Best located on south-facing roofs, photovoltaic cell panels convert sunlight to electricity. In spite of advances in research, photovoltaic energy is still too expensive to be cost-effective even in the highest utility rate areas. A 1990 residential installation might cost $20,000 or more to achieve required electrical needs, yet may be the most economical way to deliver power to homes far from utility lines. Despite the current high costs, photovoltaics is the renewable energy technology likely to advance most rapidly in the years ahead. Scientists are progressively increasing the amount of energy that photovoltaic cells capture, and lowering their costs. According to *World Watch* magazine, during the past two decades, the cost of photovoltaic power has fallen from $30.00 a kilowatt-hour to just 30 cents. The Electric Power Research Institute, a utility consortium, predicts that by the late 1990s, solar cells will become cheaper than conventional power sources in the sunny Southwest. Scientists at the U.S. Solar Energy Research Institute (SERI) estimate that photovoltaics will be capable of supplying over half of U.S. electricity in four to five decades.

A key advantage of photovoltaics is their versatility. Photovoltaic shingles already have been developed that allow a roofing material to become a power source.

WIND POWER

Wind power is one renewable energy source that came of age during the 1980s. The cost of wind energy has fallen by about 70 percent during the last decade. Today, more than 20,000 electricity-producing wind machines are in use worldwide; most of these are in the blustery mountain passes of California and in Denmark. By the year 2030, wind power could provide more than 10 to 20 percent of the world's electricity. According to *World Watch* magazine, U.S. government studies show that one quarter of the country's power could be provided by wind farms installed on the windiest 1.5 percent of the continental United States, which could replace the 18 percent of energy the U.S. receives from nuclear power plants.

Large, finely crafted windmills can generate electricity for residential use. The energy created can be stored in batteries for later use. Wind power is practical only in areas that have strong, steady winds.

COMBUSTION HEAT GENERATION

The increase in world population and the rapid deterioration of our environment place a burden on all of us to choose energy-generating systems that are ecologically sound. Until photovoltaic cells and wind-driven power become more affordable, most homeowners are dependent upon their local utility district or the companies that deliver fossil fuels for their heat generation.

WOOD

In some regions, such as the Pacific Northwest, wood is abundant at a relatively low cost. However, wood smoke is the leading cause of air pollution in winter in most western cities, according to the Environmental Protection Agency. At present, in most metropolitan areas, burning bans during stagnant-air weather systems prohibit the use of burning wood as supplemental heat.

Still, most homeowners will choose fireplaces or woodstoves because of the appeal of a wood fire; it tends to be the focus where family and friends gather. Most people know that a traditional fireplace pulls about 90 percent of the heat generated by the flames out the chimney. Airtight glass screens eliminate drafts and slow the heat loss. Wood-burning stoves, more efficient than fireplaces, are coming under fire because many people use them as a sole source of heat, producing round-the-clock pollutants.

Gas fireplaces have become an increasingly popular alternative to wood fireplaces and are far less polluting. For example, a gas-powered insert puts out .075 gram of particulate material per hour, compared with a woodstove's 7.5 grams and a wood-burning fireplace's 45 grams, according to the Gas Appliance Manufacturer's Association. For those who find the blue flame of a gas fireplace unappealing, manufacturers are now producing gas fireplaces with more realistic golden flames rising from imitation logs.

FOSSIL FUELS

Fossil fuels are the most widely used sources of energy throughout the world, but the production, transportation, and use of fossil fuels all create environmental problems. Additionally, the specter of global warming may require us to phase out fossil fuels long before Earth's limited reserves are depleted. Of the three fossil fuels available (natural gas, coal, or oil), natural gas burns most cleanly, creating fewer poisonous by-products.

But even the cleanest burning fossil fuel produces carbon dioxide, a seemingly innocuous gas that may be contributing to a phenomenon called "the greenhouse effect." Carbon dioxide, like glass in a greenhouse, allows sunlight to warm the earth but prevents heat from escaping back into space. No conclusive proof links carbon dioxide with the greenhouse effect, but circumstantial evidence has convinced many scientists that this is the cause.

ELECTRICAL HEAT GENERATION

ELECTRICAL RESISTANCE HEATING

Electricity, less efficient for heating than a combustion or flame system, is usually more costly. On a municipal level, electricity generation involves complex technology and massive environmental impacts. When nuclear power plants are used to generate electricity, disastrous accidents may occur. The escalating danger of radioactive wastes leaking from storage sites into groundwater systems threatens future generations. Also, the massive amounts of water used to cool reactor cores contribute to thermal pollution.

HEAT PUMPS

Heat pumps work especially well in moderate climates and may be combined with electrical resistance systems. A heat pump can be used for heating as well as air-conditioning when the cycle is reversed. During cold weather, the unit takes heat from outside air and brings it inside. In summer, the entire process is reversed to cool the home. Heat pumps are extremely efficient as electricity is used to run the compressor and fan only. Below 20 or 30 degrees Fahrenheit, heat pumps become no more efficient than electric resistance heating and make the most sense in mild climates where winter temperatures seldom fall below 30 degrees Fahrenheit.

Heat pumps are used widely in residences and offices. An electric forced-air system using a heat pump may cost four to six times as much as a forced-air electric heating system. However, with savings of 15 to 25 percent on their annual heating bill, most buyers can expect a payback period of about four to six years. A caveat: Inexpensive heat pumps are known for failures, so plan to buy a top-end heat pump—at 1990 prices, about $8,000.

HEAT TRANSFER SYSTEMS

Although immediate choices for ecologically sound energy-generating systems can be limited by financial considerations, the homeowner can still conserve considerable energy by paying attention to heat transfer and heat loss. Generally, the closer we are to the source of heat, the more efficient the usage will be. The heat loss that occurs in the ducts and pipes that transfer heated air and water can be reduced by efficient duct layout, proper insulation, and, wherever possible, locating the ducts in heated areas of the home.

FORCED AIR

The most popular heating system is forced air. Intake air is heated by a furnace and the warmed air is blown through a series of ducts and registers located in different areas of the home. If the registers are located in floors or at the base of walls, the principle of convection, in which warm air rises, allows for more efficient circulation. Maximum circulation can be achieved when the registers are located below outside windows. The simultaneous dropping of cold air across the window and the warm air rising from the register create a perfect exchange.

Forced-air systems generally provide fast, uniform heat. Forced-air heat pumps or high-efficiency heating systems are relatively efficient. They do, however, require large ducts to move large quantitites of heated air at acceptable velocities and noise levels (in contrast to radiant systems, which use small pipes). Also, the heated air is full of small particles that may irritate the throat and introduce carbon into breathing air. The room air temperature required to achieve the same level of comfort is higher in a forced-air system than in a radiant system. One advantage to a forced-air heat pump system is the air-cooling capabilities when operating on its air-conditioning cycle.

RADIANT SYSTEMS

In a floor radiant system, an electric heating element or hot water pipes are placed either under lightweight concrete or beneath the surface of a wooden floor. Both systems will work under lightweight carpeting. The advantages of radiant heating are: (1) it can be easily zoned (controlled to heat separate rooms to different temperatures) and offers great flexibility in installing the exact amount of heat needed; (2) it is invisible and noiseless; (3) some people feel radiant heat is more efficient because the air is not heated, rather the objects in the room and floor surface warm the occupant; and (4) it does not interfere with furniture or drapery placement. Convection also occurs in radiant heating, as the warm air rises and the cold air falls.

Radiant panels are the newest development in radiant heating design. They are installed at the baseboard level, and they rise only five inches above floor level. The panels fit easily into the wall, and they extend only one inch beyond the wall, thus making the placement of furniture easy.

Because radiant energy requires no air exchange, many homeowners use air-to-air heat exchangers to draw in fresh outside air and expel stale air. An air-to-air exchanger is able to recapture more than 80 percent of the heat in the outgoing air, transferring the warmth to the incoming fresh air.

AIR-TO-AIR HEAT EXCHANGERS

Homeowners install air-to-air heat exchangers when air exchanges are hampered, such as in a superinsulated home or a home heated with radiant energy or electric baseboard heating. Without proper outside air exchange, excessive humidity can build up and cause wood to swell, paint to peel, and mildew to grow. Air-to-air heat exchangers ventilate the home and transfer some of the heat from the warm, stale air as it leaves the house to the fresh, cooler air coming in. They also provide natural ventilation during the cooling season. An air-to-air heat exchanger is "a must" for a tight, superinsulated home.

HEAT LOSS PREVENTION AND AIR CIRCULATION

Many steps can be taken to minimize heat loss through air infiltration, such as caulking and weatherstripping around door and window frames (note that water pipe and heater insulation does not affect infiltration; see Table 2, pages 216–17). However, great care should be taken when increasing insulation and eliminating natural air infiltration. Although excessive air infiltration wastes energy, some infiltration is needed to keep healthy outside air circulating in the home. Building materials such as plywood, Swedish-finished hardwood floors, and particle board release high levels of formaldehyde and other harmful toxins. Plastic laminates, synthetic carpets, and glues are other sources of home air pollution, especially in newer homes. An air exchange is needed to vent toxins to the outside and to reduce moisture in the home.

HEAT STORAGE

Thermal efficiency and heat storage are the main components of an energy-efficient home. Mass makes an excellent container for storing heat. The trend is toward using building components that are not just useful but also attractive. Concrete floors, brick masonry, and paved floors all have a high amount of mass. These components, which can reduce energy costs if placed properly, help justify expenses that otherwise would be made solely for aesthetic appeal. By locating these components so the sun strikes them through south-facing windows, warmth will radiate into your living space long after the sun goes down.

EXERCISES

1. How do you want to heat and cool your home?

2. Do you want to incorporate another alternative energy system in your home (active or passive solar, superinsulation, heat pump, etc.)? If yes, elaborate.

3. Do you want to allow for future installation of such a system?

4. Does anyone in your family have allergies to any building materials or heat sources?

5. Do you want an electronic air cleaner?

6. In what areas do you want a fireplace or a woodstove? (Note whether it will be a primary heat source, a backup heat source, or will simply provide ambience.)

Outside wood storage is directly accessible through an interior door.

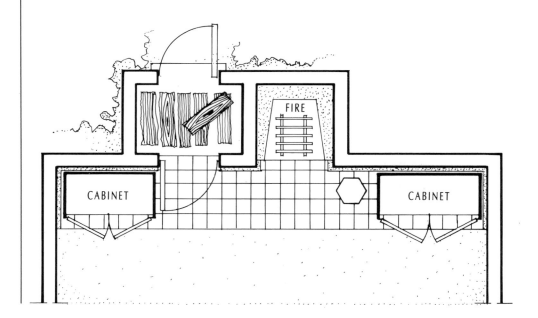

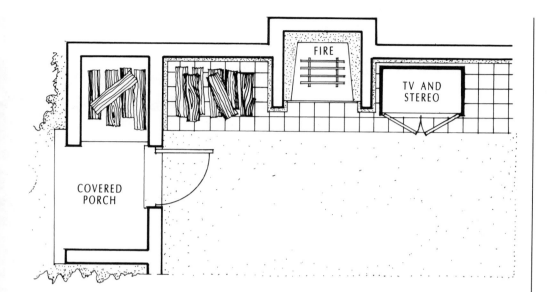

The back door provides easy access to outside wood storage.

7. Where do you want to locate your wood storage? (Wood should be kept dry and away from all other wood surfaces, to discourage bugs, while maintaining a neat appearance.)

FAMILY'S LIFESTYLE

"We shape our buildings and then they shape us."

—*Winston Churchill*

EXERCISES

1. Do you often entertain formally?

    Where do you entertain? Indoors as well as outdoors?

2. What size groups do you generally like to entertain?

3. Are separate living and dining rooms needed?

4. Is a separate kitchen needed?

5. What are your feelings regarding a "great space" (kitchen, dining, and living combined)? See page 8.

6. Is a family room needed?

   If so, do you prefer one that is

   —— open to or close to the kitchen?

   —— located in another part of the house? (Since most family rooms contain televisions, those who prefer a quiet kitchen may want it in a separate area.)

7. If you want a family room, what specific functions will it serve?

   —— TV room

   —— exercise room

   —— playroom

   —— children's party room

   —— guest room for overnight visitors

   —— other: _____

8. Do you have help with the children?

   Do any special provisions need to be made for this person?

9. Do any family members work either full-time or part-time at home? If yes, elaborate.

Will you need a separate office? (If so, list your requirements in Chapter 11, question 1.)

10. Will you often have business-related callers at your home?

If so, how will this be accommodated to maintain the privacy of your personal area? (See page 8: Note that the home office has its own separate entrance.)

11. Do you enjoy outdoor living?

What kinds of activities do you pursue outside and from which rooms do you want these areas accessible?

12. Do you anticipate that the size of your family will change (additional children, elderly parents coming to live with you, grown children moving out)? If yes, elaborate.

13. What kind of pets do you have and what provisions must be made for them?

14. What furniture, artwork, and artifacts do you wish to feature or put in special locations?

15. Do you want built-in furniture?

    If so, which rooms and what type of built-ins?

    Built-in Items   Location(s)

    bookcases   _____

                                   _____

                                   _____

    cabinets   _____

                                   _____

                                   _____

    window seats   _____

                                   _____

                                   _____

    other:_____   _____

    _____   _____

    _____   _____

16. In which rooms do you want to watch TV? Describe your treatment
    and functions on the following page:

a. TV completely exposed
b. TV built into cabinet
c. TV in stand-alone furniture unit
d. standard TV size
e. large-screen TV
f. VCR and tape storage

Rooms   *Functions/Treatment*

_____   _____

_____   _____

_____   _____

_____   _____

_____   _____

Note: If an outside antenna is to be installed, run wire to all desired TV locations before drywall work begins.

17. In which rooms or outdoor spaces do you want to hear music? Where do you want to locate the controls?

Natural light from a stairwell skylight accents and brightens a curved stair landing.

18. Describe a typical workday in the life of your family.

19. Describe a typical weekend day in the life of your family.

5

FOR THE REMODELER

"It is something to be able to paint a particular picture or to carve a statue, and so to make a few objects beautiful, but it is far more glorious to carve and paint the very atmosphere and medium through which we look. . . . To affect the quality of the day—that is the highest of arts."

—Henry David Thoreau

. . . .

REMODELING VS. MOVING OR BUILDING NEW

Many readers will be remodeling rather than building a new home. While you may simply complete this chapter and the one pertinent to the rooms to be remodeled, we advise that you also complete Chapters 1, 3, 4, and 16, and the relevant questions in Chapter 2. They contain exercises that will help ensure that the remodel truly meets the needs of the entire household and is kept within your budget.

If you are designing a new home from scratch, skip this chapter and proceed with the remaining chapters.

When a house feels too small for comfort, it's exciting to think about adding on. The first question to ask yourself is: Does it make sense for your family, your house, your neighborhood, and your finances to invest in an addition? Are you willing to tolerate major inconvenience or live in another place during construction? Many homeowners remark that living in a house during a major remodeling project is one of the most stressful experiences ever encountered. Can you live with workers walking throughout your home, storing building materials where you normally park and live, and with the endless dust and noise? If you're remodeling your kitchen, you'll need to add to the list of inconveniences: no place to cook or eat, and nowhere to wash dishes except in the bathtub. Planning and remodeling a home sometimes can be as complex as planning an entirely new house.

Perhaps the problem is one that could be more easily solved with more efficient storage systems, or by reworking the space you already have. Ask yourself if every room is being fully utilized. See if you can search out underused spaces. Even skillful decorating can make rooms appear larger.

There are certainly many reasons to consider remodeling instead of relocating, including the increased cost of both real estate and new housing and the elimination of moving and relocation costs (as well as commissions and closing costs). The more important reasons may be emotional ones: keeping children in a familiar school system and maintaining treasured neighborhood friendships.

The before photo of the house pictured on page 66.

If you are thinking about embarking on a major remodeling project, it would be wise to consult with an architect and a contractor about your general plans. In a one- to two-hour consultation, an architect can advise you whether it makes more sense to build up or build out (if your property setbacks are acceptable). Neither the architect nor a contractor can be 100 percent accurate about costs for a remodel: No one knows what hidden conditions will be encountered behind closed walls. A contractor's fixed bid likely will be inflated with contingencies for unknown factors. This may be a good case for a cost-plus job (refer to Chapter 16, "Getting It Done on Budget"). In all cases, you must follow local building, electrical, fire, and zoning codes.

The National Association of Home Builders recommends that the current market value of your home, plus the remodeling cost, should not be more than 20 percent greater than the top value of comparable homes in your neighborhood. The following exercises will help you determine if a house remodel is the route for you.

CHECKLIST

(No response is required. These are standard items that should not be overlooked.)

1. Does the exterior design of the remodel complement the existing home, landscaping, and neighborhood?

2. Does the interior of the remodel tie in with the household's traffic patterns and mechanical systems?

EXERCISES

REASONS TO REMODEL VS. MOVING

1. What are your reasons for wanting to remodel?

    _____ good neighborhood

    _____ good schools

    _____ proximity to work

    _____ proximity to amenities

    _____ beautiful view

    _____ beautiful site

    _____ many good features about your home:

    _____

    _____

    _____

    _____

    _____

_____ other reasons (your home's bad points):

_____

_____

_____

_____

_____

2. Describe how you want your home to change. (Examples: more square footage, a new kitchen, more open space, more private areas, an attractive exterior, more natural light, improved circulation.)

HOME'S PRESENT CONDITION

3. What is your home's physical condition? (The best candidate for a remodel is a home that is structurally sound.)

	Very Good	Good	Fair	Poor
Is the foundation in good shape?	____	____	____	____
How about the interior walls and floors?	____	____	____	____
What is the condition of the roof and the exterior?	____	____	____	____
Windows?	____	____	____	____
Heating/cooling system?	____	____	____	____
Electrical system?	____	____	____	____
Plumbing system?	____	____	____	____
Insulation and energy efficiency?	____	____	____	____

4. Does your home contain asbestos or any other hazardous materials?

5. Describe your home's present heating/cooling system.

Can it reach the proposed areas of your remodel?

NEIGHBORHOOD

6. Describe your neighborhood. Would an addition overprice your home for the neighborhood?

7. Is your home in a Historic Preservation District? If so, what are the requirements that will affect your home?

PRACTICALITIES

8. Have you checked with a bank to see if your proposed budget is feasible?

   Are they willing to finance it? (Refer to Chapter 16, "Getting It Done on Budget," for cost estimating.)

9. Does your site have room for a ground-level expansion?

If not, will you need to build up?

Will going up provide you with a view?

Have you checked local zoning ordinances to see what is possible? (The questions in Chapter 2, "Site Conditions," address the major legal concerns.)

INTERIOR STRUCTURAL CHANGES

10. Have you considered removing any interior walls? If so, which ones? (By removing walls, you can often alter your house dramatically. If

the wall you are thinking about removing is load bearing, a structural beam will be required.)

11. Have you considered removing a ceiling? (You may lose space from your attic, or the room above, but you can often let in more sunlight and create larger volume spaces that make your home's interior appear bigger. Before you remove any joists, beams, or trusses, consult an architect or contractor.)

12. Have you considered adding a bay window? (Creating a bay is ideal for a room that is small and dark.)

If so, where?

Do you want to include seating area in the bay window?

13. Have you considered adding a dormer?

RENOVATING LESS-COSTLY AREAS

14. Have you considered the four most logical, and least costly, renovating areas—basement, attic, garage, or porch? (The garage, basement, and attic are often three big space wasters—and the structural elements for a remodel are already in place.)

The pros and cons of each area will be addressed, but first, rate the structural condition of each:

	Very Good	Good	Fair	Poor	Not Applicable
attic	_____	_____	_____	_____	_____
basement	_____	_____	_____	_____	_____
garage	_____	_____	_____	_____	_____
porch	_____	_____	_____	_____	_____

15. Do you want to remodel your basement? If so, answer the following questions.

Does the basement have adequate headroom (7′6″ minimum)?

Does the basement have moisture problems? (Often a damp basement can be dried out by using interior or exterior waterproofing, a dehumidifier, or improved exterior drainage.)

Does your basement have adequate natural lighting?

Is your basement heated?

Does your basement have adequate ventilation?

Is the access to your basement satisfactory?

Would an exterior staircase make it easier to reach a backyard patio or deck?

Do you want to convert your basement into

_____ a self-contained apartment? (If so, check your local zoning ordinances and building codes.)

_____ a multipurpose workshop?

_____ a home office or study? (This can be an ideal location because it is quiet and removed from the main activity areas of the home.)

_____ a recreation room?

_____ sleeping space? (If so, basement windows must provide safe and legal egress.)

16. When space is at a premium, devoting an entire attic to old furniture and storage is a waste of your home's resources. Often, by adding a ventilating skylight, windows on end walls, or a dormer, an attic can be used for added living space. If you want to remodel your attic, answer the following questions.

What is the existing ceiling height? (In most regions, if the attic is to be used as living space, the headroom height must be 7'6" over half of its floor space. You may be able to solve the height problem by adding a dormer or two.)

Do your attic joists need strengthening before putting in a finished floor?

Do you need to add insulation for year-round warmth?

Is your attic heated?

Does your attic have adequate ventilation? (Frequently, this can be solved by adding a circulating fan.)

Do you need to relocate the access? (If you plan to use your attic space for sleeping, you must provide for egress windows and a secondary escape route for fire safety.)

17. For a garage conversion, turning a one-job area into a living space can be tempting (because the structure is essentially complete), particularly if your budget is tight and you don't mind parking your car in the street or driveway. If you want to remodel your garage, answer the following questions.

    Is your garage structurally sound and dry?

    Where else can you park your car(s)?

    Which utilities are already connected?

    How do you plan to use your remodeled garage space?

    If your garage is detached, have you considered adding a room between your house and garage?

18. A porch that is used infrequently can be enclosed, insulated, and even expanded to become a sunroom or an extension of the living area.

The advantage of a porch conversion is cost savings, because most of your structural elements already exist: foundations, floor, posts, and roof. Do you want to consider enclosing your porch?

Does it have an adequate foundation for increased structural loads?

REMODELING THE KITCHEN

19. The kitchen is the room most often remodeled. If you want to remodel or add to your kitchen, answer the following questions and the ones in the chapter on kitchens.

Why do you want to remodel your kitchen?

—— more room

—— more counter space

—— more storage space

—— an eating area

—— new appliances

—— more natural light

—— more artificial light

—— better ventilation

—— improved circulation

—— more contemporary appearance

—— more efficient layout

—— other: _____

_____

_____

Before: This dark, cramped kitchen was a good candidate for a remodel.

Have you considered the existing plumbing lines and where they would be relocated? (Generally, moving a sink a few feet in either direction is not costly, but moving it across a room can be.)

Do you want to move your refrigerator? (If so, you will need a space that is convenient, can accommodate its bulk, and is wired for 120 volts.)

Do you want to move your range? (This requires ventilation and 220 volts.)

After: Expanding outward and adding a skylight above the sink allowed the owners to enjoy a larger and more open kitchen. Note that the double-Dutch door on the right provides convenient access to a new patio area.

6

KITCHEN AND DINING AREAS

"The kitchen is . . . the hub of the home. It is not only the place where we cook, eat, and entertain . . . it is also the place where the children gather and play. It really ought to be renamed the 'living room,' because that is what it is."

—Terence Conran,
The Kitchen Book

CHECKLIST

(No response is required. These are standard items that should not be overlooked.)

1. Is there easy access from garage to kitchen (for example, with a load of groceries)?

2. Is the triangular distance from the sink to the stove to the refrigerator and back to the sink (the "work triangle") between twelve and twenty-one feet? (See pages 89–90.)

3. Is your kitchen arranged so that family traffic does not interfere with the "work triangle"?

4. Can a cook with a boiling pot of pasta get from the cooktop to the sink—very quickly—without an island or other obstacle impeding the footpath?

5. Is there "toe space" under all cabinets?

6. Are there special lights for sink, range, and food preparation and mixing areas so that you never work in your own shadow?

7. If undercabinet lights are used, are they installed on the forward edge of the upper cabinet bottoms? (This gives better task illumination and results in less glare on work surfaces.)

8. Have you allowed a minimum of two feet of counter on either side of the sink, two feet on either side of the range, and eighteen inches next to the handle side of your refrigerator?

9. Is the microwave oven installed between countertop and eye level, about forty-two to forty-four inches off the floor?

10. Have you allowed sufficient counter space near the microwave oven for a hot dish to be quickly set down?

11. Is there a mixing counter at least three feet long?

12. Have you allowed a minimum of ten feet of cabinet frontage below counter height and seven feet above for average storage needs?

13. Are dish and flatware storage areas close to the dishwasher for easy unloading?

14. Are storage areas directly related to activity areas? For example, are pots and pans stored underneath the cooktop? Are mixing bowls and baking equipment kept near the baking center? Are cookie sheets near the oven?

15. Have you allowed a minimum of 3′ for clear passage throughout the kitchen? (This is particularly important if two or more people will be preparing meals at the same time.)

16. Have you considered the problems of a western exposure for the kitchen? (Western afternoon sun comes in at a near horizontal angle in the summer; it's difficult to control and can overheat the kitchen.)

17. Have you located a window next to the kitchen sink? (This will help make cleaning up a more enjoyable task.)

18. Have you located the pantry away from direct sunlight to help guard against possible food spoilage?

19. Can the refrigerator be opened without disrupting someone else who may be preparing a meal?

20. Is the dining table light on a dimmer switch?

21. If young children will be in the kitchen, does the garbage disposal operate only when the safety lid is in place?

An open and airy kitchen
provides the owners with
a view of Puget Sound.

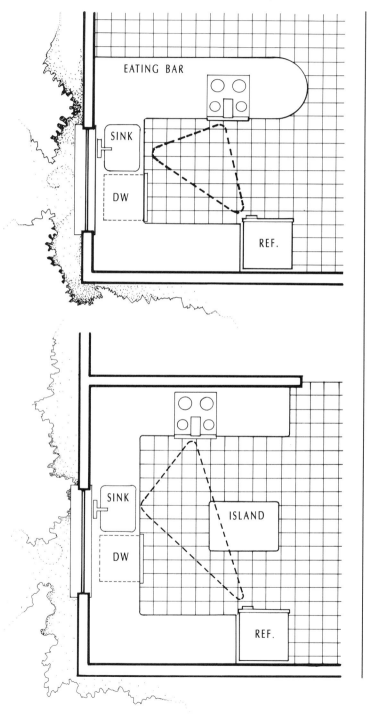

EATING BAR

SINK

DW

REF.

U-shaped kitchen with peninsula. Pull up a chair and watch the cook in action. The U-shaped plan is usually the most efficient and desirable arrangement for many kitchens. Note that the work triangle is kept to a minimum distance between the most frequently used appliances. If you plan to use a plastic laminate countertop, install a small area of tile next to your cooktop, to place hot pots and pans.

SINK

ISLAND

DW

REF.

Island kitchen. This work triangle is a little longer than the one above, but the island is convenient for placing food after removing it from the refrigerator, for fresh-washed vegetables from the sink, or even as a baking center. If you plan to use your island as a baking center, install an electrical outlet on the island cabinet face.

L-shaped kitchen. This arrangement works well on two adjacent walls. It's not as convenient as the kitchens on the previous page, but is the next best choice.

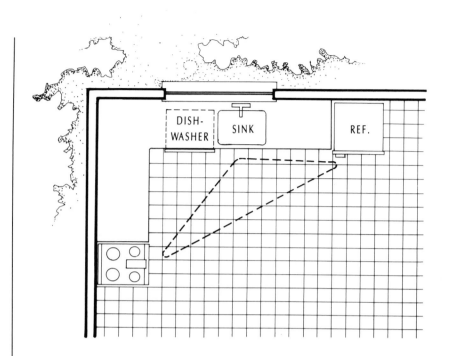

Galley kitchen. This is the least desirable of the work triangles, but sometimes is the only option. The disadvantage is that it frequently has a corridor feel, and if the walls are enclosed, it does not feel open. A wall separating the kitchen from the dining space is a good place to install a "pass-through."

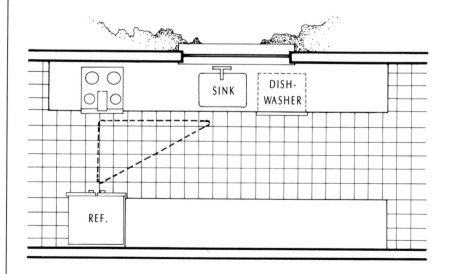

EXERCISES

INDIVIDUAL KITCHEN NEEDS

1. Do you want your kitchen on the east side of your home? (Many people enjoy preparing and eating breakfast in the morning sunlight.)

2. Are you a one-cook, two-cook, or "everyone join in" type of family?

3. Do several people clean up simultaneously or does one person?

4. Are you a quick, practical cook or do you enjoy preparing elaborate meals?

5. Do you want the kitchen to share space with an informal dining area?

If so, what function will it serve?

____ breakfast/quick meals

____ afternoon tea

____ casual conversation

Should the area include a table or an eating bar?

If you want a place for friends to sit while you're cooking but budget or space limitations do not permit an informal dining table, consider installing a two-person built-in cushioned seat with broad arm rests (8 inches wide is recommended) to accommodate drinks or snacks.

6. Where do you prefer to serve breakfast?

____ in the kitchen

____ in the dining room

____ in the family room

____ at a counter in the kitchen or family room

____ in a special breakfast nook

7. Do you want a kitchen desk to plan menus, schedule, organize grocery lists, and handle bills and correspondence?

Should this be open to view or partially to fully screened?

Do you want a filing drawer?

A sunny breakfast area links an open kitchen to a wooded glen outside the greenhouse window.

8. Do you want a bulletin board for posting important flyers, notices, and reminders?

9. Do you want a message board next to your kitchen phone?

10. Do you want a mixing center?

11. Do you do a lot of baking?

    Do you want a separate lower marble surface for pastry making?

    If so, do you want a flour bin drawer underneath?

12. Describe how and where you prefer to store your spices (some people prefer two spice racks: one for baking, the other one for cooking).

13. Do you want a separate pantry?

14. Do you want any open shelves/storage in your kitchen for display and easy access?

15. Do you want any pullout shelves in your base cabinets?

16. Do you want a revolving corner cabinet? (It is practical, yet more expensive than a standard cabinet.)

17. Do you want high storage to keep things out of the reach of children?

18. Do you want a broom closet in your kitchen?

19. The standard height of kitchen counters is thirty-six inches. Do you want counters that are

    _____ higher than standard?
    _____ lower than standard?

20. Do you want one kitchen counter six inches deeper than the others? (Some people prefer a deeper counter on the wall that is flush with the refrigerator, or along a wall that contains an appliance garage.)

21. Do you have any special requirements for wine storage? (Wine requires a constant temperature, darkness, and an absence of vibration. Bottles should be stored so the cork remains moist.)

SINK OPTIONS

Stainless steel is easy to clean and durable. Its disadvantage is noise.

Enameled cast iron will not scratch, stain, dent, chip, or cause any clatter.

Synthetic sinks (such as Fountainhead® by Nevamor) can be sculpted to tie in with countertop materials as a one-piece assembly, with no caulking to disintegrate or become discolored.

A double-bowled sink is advisable for doing dishes.

The treble sink, even more efficient, includes an extra bowl for the waste disposer, so that rubbish and dishes never coincide and utensils are not sucked into the garbage disposal.

22. What type of sink do you prefer (size, number of compartments, and material)?

23. Do you want two sinks in your kitchen?

If so, where? (Some cooks prefer a second sink, for washing vegetables, near the chopping block area. Locate this sink away from the main sink so two people have room to prepare meals easily. The second sink could double as a bar sink.)

24. For your sink area, rank on a 1 to 4 scale (1 = most important, 4 = least important) the following features:

____ spray attachments

____ instant hot water

____ dispenser for liquid soap

____ dispenser for lotion

KITCHEN ELECTRICAL OUTLETS

Basic recommendations include locating a duplex outlet every four feet, a duplex in the kitchen island, and a four-plex near the serving counter.

A plug strip along one countertop wall is also helpful. If you want an appliance garage, allow adequate outlets for all your appliances.

25. Do you have any special requirements for the placement of electrical outlets in your kitchen?

KITCHEN APPLIANCES

New technologies make customizing your kitchen easier, but before deciding on a particular appliance, consider present and future needs, space limitations, energy consumption, and the options available. Whenever you shop for a major appliance, look for the bright yellow Energy Guide label for energy-use comparisons.

Before deciding on a range or an oven with a separate cooktop, your first decision will be whether you prefer gas or electric. Professional chefs prefer gas. The flame provides a visual cue and more responsive temperature control. Newer models use electric ignitors in place of pilot lights, eliminating the constant flow of gas. The primary danger in using gas is carbon monoxide poisoning, produced when fuels do not burn completely. All fuel-burning appliances need air for the fuel to burn efficiently. When there is inadequate ventilation (such as in the superinsulated home) or the appliance is not operating properly, carbon monoxide is produced and can gradually overcome an unsuspecting bystander. If you are committed to cooking with gas, a smart compromise is an electric oven and a gas cooktop with sealed gas burners, making cleanup easier.

Electric Cooktops

The popularity of cooktops continues to grow with the greater choice of heat-transference methods. Newer advances in electric equipment offer more precise heat adjustment. Also, many modular cooktops are equipped with rotisseries, griddles, deep fryers, and grills. Here are your options:

1. *Electric elements* (least expensive)—Traditional coils can be difficult to clean. The newer "hob" tops (cast-iron disks) heat up slowly but retain their heat, so cooking continues even after the burner has been turned off.

2. *Halogen* (more expensive)—Safely protected under a glass ceramic top, halogen lamps produce heat almost instantly. They respond quickly to power level changes. Glass ceramic cooktops are energy-efficient and easy to clean.

3. *Magnetic induction* (most expensive)—Electromagnetic energy is transferred directly to cookware (cast iron, stainless steel, enameled iron, etc.) through a glass cooking surface that heats and cooks food. There are no open flames or hot coils; the surface won't burn you if touched accidentally. The burners automatically shut off once the pot is removed, a boon for easily distracted cooks. Magnetic induction burners are energy-efficient and also offer very good temperature control.

Ranges and Ovens

Even with today's many choices for cooktop options, there are reasons to choose a range. You might need the cabinet space a wall oven would occupy. Also, a range can cost 10 to 20 percent less than installing a cooktop with a separate built-in oven. If you prefer to do all your cooking in one location, a range is ideal. For safety, be sure the controls are located at the front rather than on the backsplash.

Commercial ranges and ovens are engineered to operate for ten or twelve hours at a time and are not efficient for home use. Some new commercial-style ranges designed for residential use weigh less, fit smaller spaces, and combine efficient gas cooktops with electric ovens without compromising aesthetic or functional benefits, but often require expensive venting systems.

Whether you opt for a built-in oven or a range, you will have to decide about the following options:

1. *Conventional*—These ovens are the most common and least expensive. They heat up the kitchen, but are ideal for baking. If young children are in the kitchen, choose a model with a double-insulated door.

2. *Convection*—These ovens use fans to circulate heat. They heat up faster at lower temperatures, making them more energy-efficient, and do not throw off as much heat in the kitchen as conventional ovens.

3. *Microwave*—These ovens use high-frequency radio waves to bombard food, causing molecules to move rapidly. This friction quickly heats and cooks the food. Spills wipe up easily and no heat is generated. A microwave oven is not a substitute for a regular oven, particularly if you bake or roast frequently. Microwave ovens are time-efficient and come in a variety of sizes with options. A microwave oven uses 30 to 70 percent less energy than a conventional oven.

The microwave oven should be adjacent to the refrigerator in the food preparation area. A second practical location is above or adjacent to the cooktop. Avoid placing the microwave over the oven as it is usually too far away from where the cook works.

4. *CMT*—A microwave tube on the top works independently from or simultaneously with electric bake and broil elements, allowing users to cook and brown foods quickly. This is an expensive option.

Refrigerators

The main considerations are capacity, energy efficiency, and whether you need a left- or right-hand door. Several manufacturers offer 24-inch-deep refrigerators that may be installed flush with the kitchen cabinets. Special panels that match the cabinets may be purchased for the refrigerator's doors. A side-by-side refrigerator is a good option if you do not have a separate freezer. One disadvantage is that it is more difficult to store large-size platters. Side-by-side units usually offer more shelf configurations and tend to be more deluxe in appearance and features. If you require an ice maker, make sure that you have the water piped to your refrigerator location.

Dishwashers

When comparing models, look at capacity, quietness, loading ease, and no-heat or low-heat drying cycles that save energy. Some other options you should consider: liquid rinse dispensers to counteract the spotting effect of unusually hard water; food pulverizers that grind up and dispose of soft food; delicate cycles to protect china; programmable start times that allow you to run the unit at convenient hours; automatic temperature monitors that signal the dishwasher to operate only after the water has been heated to an optimum of 140 degrees Fahrenheit.

Large and Small Appliances

26. What features (or brands and model names) do you want in your large appliances? (Specify gas or electric for cooktop and oven.)

Large Appliances	Features (or brand/model)
range or cooktop	_____
separate oven	_____
refrigerator	_____
dishwasher	_____
garbage disposal	_____
microwave oven	_____
trash compactor*	_____
other: _____	_____

*Consider installing recycling bins instead. Trash compactors inhibit the natural breakdown of garbage at the disposal site, and the unit can quickly become odoriferous and attract vermin.

27. What small appliances will you be using and where do you want to put them? Some small appliances you may want to consider are a toaster, toaster oven, coffee unit, electric can opener, food processor, mixmaster, and juicer. (If you choose an appliance compartment, or appliance garage, allow a 30-inch countertop in that area so you don't lose countertop space.)

Small Appliances	Appliance Garage	Countertop	Other Space
_____	_____	_____	_____
_____	_____	_____	_____
_____	_____	_____	_____
_____	_____	_____	_____
_____	_____	_____	_____

RECYCLING

Taking out the trash was once a mere inconvenience. Now, it has burgeoned into a national ecological threat. The average American generates 3.5 pounds of trash a day—1,277 pounds a year—which adds up to 5,108 pounds a year for a family of four.

Half of what goes into landfills can be recycled. A significant reduction in waste can be attained by recycling. In Japan, for example, only 24 percent of the total volume of trash ends up in landfills; the other 76 percent is recycled.

Recycling bins and drawers must be aesthetic and easy to empty and clean or they will not be practical. They should also be located near the use site. For example, the compost bin should be close to the vegetable cutting surface.

The simplest plan uses a wide or deep drawer—twenty-four inches deep by thirteen inches wide by twenty inches high, for example (see opposite)—designed to hold three paper grocery bags. This provides one

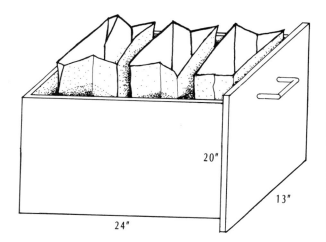

20"

13"

24"

Family recycling habits are encouraged by a recycling drawer in the kitchen. This inexpensive system uses ordinary paper grocery bags.

holding place each for glass, aluminum, and metal. When full, or on pickup days, the bags merely have to be lifted out. Heavy-duty, full-extension drawer runners should be used.

Dual-access recycling cabinets are another option. These are cabinets that can be reached from front and back, facilitating both the storage of recyclables from the kitchen side and their removal from an adjacent area, such as a mud room, foyer, or hall. This design works well in high-rise apartments and houses without basements.

Some families prefer to store recyclables outside their home in a well-protected area or in a garage.

28. If your family recycles waste material, describe what would work most conveniently for you. (Some families like (a) an opening in their chopping block for organic matter that will be going to the compost pile, and (b) a temporary place to put glass, aluminum, and metal before taking it out to the larger recycling receptacles in the garage.)

LIGHTING AND OTHER KITCHEN FEATURES

29. How do you prefer to light your kitchen? (Consider windows, sky-lights, ambient, task, and accent lighting. You may want to refer to Tables 5 and 6 on lighting.)

30. Describe what other features you want in your kitchen.

    ____ woodburning stove

    ____ cookbook display area

    ____ built-in TV

    ____ special display shelves for china, glass, or pottery

    ____ adjacent greenhouse

    ____ counter top herb garden

    ____ other: _____

    ____ other: _____

DINING ROOM

31. What are the dimensions of your dining table?

    How many does it seat?

    How many people do you want to seat on special occasions?

32. Do you want to allow for special furniture in your dining room such as a sideboard or china cabinet?

33. Do you want a storage area near your dining room for

    ——— table leaves

    ——— large serving pieces

    ——— table linen

    ——— silver

    ——— other equipment

34. How do you prefer to light your dining room?

If your budget must be cut, what compromises are acceptable?

7

THE LIVING AREA AND ENTRY

"A living room . . . confronts
each visitor with a style,
a secular faith; he compares its dogmas
with his, and decides whether
he would like to see more of us."

—W. H. Auden, "The Common Life,"
a poem from About the House

CHECKLIST

(No response is required. These are standard items that should not be overlooked.)

1. Is the front entry protected from rain and wind by a covered porch or roof extension?

2. Can a caller be seen without opening the front door?

3. Does the entry have a hard-surfaced, easily cleaned floor covering such as ceramic tile or Swedish-finish hardwood floors?

4. Is there a guest coat closet near the entry?

5. Is there a coat closet for family members near the garage or the most common entrance?

This entry provides separation and a transition into the living area.

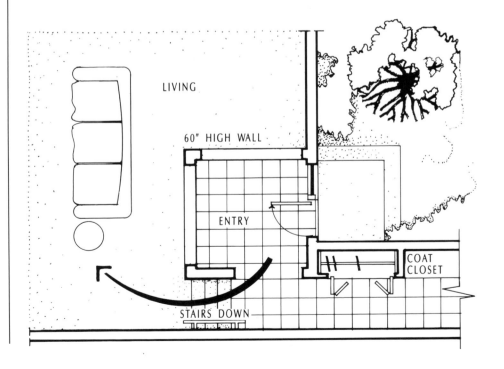

LIVING

60" HIGH WALL

ENTRY

COAT CLOSET

STAIRS DOWN

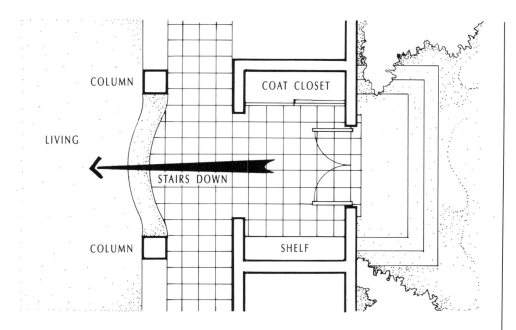

COLUMN

LIVING

COAT CLOSET

STAIRS DOWN

COLUMN

SHELF

A dramatic, unobstructed view of Puget Sound, seen through a living room picture window, is directly visible from this entry.

EXERCISES

ENTRANCES

1. Do you want a visual separation between the entry and the living area? (See pages 108 and 109 for two alternatives.)

2. How do you prefer to view a caller at the front door?

   _____ glass panel(s) in the door

   _____ glass panel(s) next to the door

   _____ a window providing a view of the front entrance

   _____ a peephole viewer built into the door

   _____ remote camera

3. Do you want special storage either inside or outside the entrance, besides the coat closet? (Some people want a small, protected storage compartment outside their homes to place items that can be picked up when they are not at home. Also, a storage shelf near the inside and/or outside entry is convenient for placing a heavy parcel while unlocking the front door.)

4. Do you want sitting space for anyone to put on or take off boots in the entry area? (This is particularly useful for children or the elderly.)

5. Do guests remove shoes upon entering your home?

   If so, do you want extra space to store the shoes?

6. What type of floor covering do you prefer to put in your front entrance? (Two easy-care suggestions are ceramic tile and Swedish-finish hardwood floors.)

LIVING SPACES

7. Describe the function of the living room in your home. Is it a place for adults only, adults and children, or is it a special occasion room? (If you have children and do not have space for both a family room and a living room, we suggest making your living room a place

where children will feel welcome. Provide a cabinet to store a few special games and tuck in some of their magazines with yours.)

8. Do you prefer seating arrangements that are conducive to formal discussions or more intimate conversation?

9. Is your living room a place where you would like a window seat, a bay window, or a large picture window?

10. Do you prefer your living space to focus outward on a view or inward on a fireplace or art display?

11. Do you want a patio door to provide access to a patio or deck?

12. What activities will take place in your living area? Check all that apply.

　　___ entertaining

　　___ club or business meetings

---- playing a piano or other musical instrument

---- listening to music

---- reading

---- watching TV

---- studying

---- playing with children

---- other: _____

13. What type of storage facilities or space should be allocated?

    ---- stereo equipment/records/tapes/CDs

    ---- camera equipment, photos, slide projector, and screen

    ---- television

    ---- toys/games

    ---- desk

    ---- bookshelves

    ---- piano or other musical instrument

    ---- art display

    ---- firewood

    ---- wet bar

    ---- other: _____

14. Where do you want to put your Christmas tree?

How tall a tree do you usually buy?

15. Describe all pieces of furniture, lamps, and area rugs that will go in your living area. Specific dimensions are needed. (Before working

drawings begin, make sure your design professional has allowed adequate room for comfortable circulation.)

Will an electrical outlet be needed in the floor of your living area? If so, for which lamps?

16. How do you prefer to light your living area? (Examples are recessed ceiling light fixtures, table lamps, wall sconces, and accent lighting. Spotlights are best aimed at artwork or the ceiling to bounce an indirect light into the room.)

If your budget must be cut, what compromises are acceptable for your living area?

8

BEDROOMS

"It seems sadly incongruous that the bedroom, which is by far the most personal room in the house, is also the most neglected. The reason, I suspect, is that it is not usually on public view, and this becomes an excuse for taking shortcuts in design and planning."

—Terence Conran

. . . .

Bedrooms provide the first images of the day; we are most vulnerable and most open as we awaken. Locating the bedroom on the eastern side to receive "wake-up" light can be an inspiring way to greet the day and provide weather information. Care should be taken, however, that sunlight does not fall directly on the bed, thus jangling the occupants awake with its harsh glare. Instead, bring in the light through an eastern window across a wall at the end of the room. Let it fall on a vase filled with fresh flowers, a sculpture, or a comfortable chair. Simple detailing and uncluttered surfaces are most restful and gently ease us into the day.

A skylight can create a wonderful atmosphere in the bedroom, capturing a moonbeam through the room as soft words and love are shared. A blackout shade on the skylight prevents bright sunlight from uncomfortably awakening sleepers.

Acoustical separation may be enhanced by locating closets, cabinets, or bookshelves between the master bedroom and other occupied spaces. A less expensive solution might include wrapping sound-deadening material between the wall studs.

For many people, especially those with young children, the bedroom is a private sanctuary, a needed retreat from being too available. A reading area, a view into an enclosed garden, natural lighting, and a privacy lock offer much needed "time out" for parents.

CHECKLIST

(No response is required. These are standard items that should not be overlooked.)

1. Are bedrooms located on the quiet side of the house, as far as possible from the main entrance and the nearest road?

2. Are bedrooms situated so they will receive eastern ("wake-up") light?

3. Are beds located so that morning sun will not shine directly onto them?

4. Are windows located to allow for cross-ventilation?

5. Are clothes closets a minimum of two feet deep?

6. Have you allowed twelve to eighteen feet of closet space in the master bedroom?

7. Have you allowed six to eight feet of closet space per person in each of the other bedrooms?

8 Have you allowed fifteen inches of open space along both sides of the bed (for ease in making the bed)?

9. Are young children's bedrooms close enough to the master bedroom so the children can be heard at night? If not, is there an intercom installed?

10. Is the bedroom close to a bathroom?

11. Are bathroom plumbing and other noise generators (older children, TV, stereo) acoustically separated from the master bedroom?

12. Can the bedrooms be safely evacuated directly to the outside in the event of a fire?

13. Is there enough wall space next to your windows to allow for full operation of draperies (if desired)?

14. If a light fixture is used above a full-length dressing room mirror, has it been positioned to shine on the person and not on the mirror?

15. Are the master bedroom light fixtures on dimmer switches?

EXERCISES

ADULT BEDROOMS

Lighting

1. Do you generally like a light or dark bedroom?

   Would you prefer the option for either?

2. Do you prefer a cozy, confined sleeping area for your bed?

3. How do you prefer to light your master bedroom? (Examples are recessed incandescent lighting or indirect lighting, where the bulbs are hidden behind a ceiling or wall cove.)

4. How frequently do you read in bed?

5. Do you want one reading light per person?

If so, do you want a wall-mounted fixture to leave the bedside free?

6. Do you want an on-off switch by the door and another by the bed so you will never have to get out of bed to turn off the lights?

7. Do you have any special requirements for the placement of electrical outlets in your bedroom?

8. Do you want to control all of the main lights in your house from your bed? (This feature is surprisingly inexpensive.)

Furnishings

9. Do you want a sitting/relaxing area?

10. Do you want a desk/study area?

11. Will any family member require a bed longer than the average seventy-two to seventy-four inches?

12. Will any family member be sleeping on a waterbed?

Special Features

13. Do you want a wood-burning stove or fireplace in your bedroom?

14. Do both partners have the same schedule? Should the master bath/ dressing area be designed to allow one person to shower, dress, and leave without waking the other?

15. Do you want a private deck?

16. Describe any other special features you want in your master bedroom.

If your budget must be cut, what compromises are acceptable?

CHILDREN'S BEDROOMS

"A preciously designed room, too perfect to touch, seems to me a difficult place for a child to grow up. The chaos added by the child makes it his or her private territory, a refuge from the adult world."
—Alan Buchsbaum, architect

A child's bedroom is a special place: It should be filled with as much fun and imagination as possible. A child's curiosity and propensity for fantasy will travel into every cubic inch of the room's volume. The room, therefore, must fulfill much more than the basic needs of sleeping, storing, studying, and recovering from illness.

An active relationship with the outside elements is encouraged when the room has generous natural light and ventilation. There should be adequate acoustical isolation to prevent the child's bellowing or screeching from incurring the wrath of a stern-faced parent working on taxes.

Finishes and furnishings should be up to the rough-and-tumble many

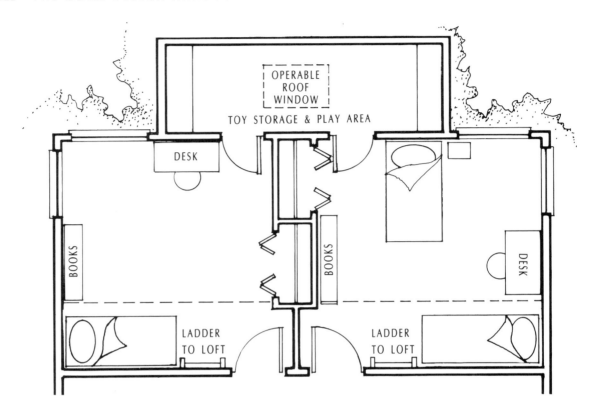

The "found" space under a pitched roof can provide a shelf-lined toy storage and play area that connects the children's bedrooms. A ladder in each bedroom climbs to private play lofts above.

children enjoy, allowing Captain Hook plenty of room to plunder and search for treasures. Where opportunity exists, incorporate a ladder up to a play loft. (See above.) Ceiling heights in these areas need not exceed four feet for crawling cave dwellers; children love small, cozy spaces.

The most ideal flooring for children is not wall-to-wall carpeting but a combination of hard surface and carpet. Young children take to the floor; everything happens there. Provide hard surfaces for their messes and an area rug for their cozy reading and board game times.

You may want to separate areas for sleep, play, and study. When possible, provide an extra bed for an overnight guest. If there's more than one child, perhaps a secret passage through a toy storage area could connect their rooms. (See above.) For children who will be sharing a bedroom, the privacy of each child can be protected by furnishings and dividers.

Although little children love short doors, low windows, and "secret" getaways, consider adaptability in your design. The most economical designs are simple and remain functional as the child grows. Everything should be reachable and adjustable. As the child grows taller, so should the closet hanging rods. Provide lots of open shelves and storage space.

No need to be subtle with finishes: bright colors, interesting textures, supergraphics, and lots of tack-up wall space will provide a supportive backdrop for creative displays of art, posters, dried leaves, and shadow puppets. Horizontal surfaces should be kept low with room for ant farms, comic books, frog aquariums, hamster cages, crayons, and kazoos.

As children age, storing clutter is best handled when nagging is kept to a minimum. Provide lots of easy-access storage bins and shelving. Children are more apt to keep their play areas neat when storage is accessible.

A teenager's room is a sanctuary, a private place to study, reflect on life, and mull over ideas. Teenagers repeatedly tell us that they value their privacy above all else. Make sure you provide an area for private phone conversations!

Designing a child's bedroom is great fun. Don't forget to consult with all children involved, including the one behind your own smile. Try to remember your own favorite spaces as a child. Remember the afternoons you spent reorganizing your parents' furniture into tents with the help of blankets? Children love small, cozy spaces where they feel enclosed in their own private world. To encourage a sense that the room is theirs, enlist their effort in its design and, where possible, construction and finishing. Children love to build! Let them help with their play structures. The room should reflect, as much as possible, the child's own interests, ideas, and feelings.

Last, but not least: Hang pictures and clocks at a child's viewing level. The child's room is his own little house in miniature and should provide for many of the same needs the house fills for the adult.

17. What are the ages of your children? Check the activities that will take place in your children's bedrooms. (Most of the activities in the list below are excerpted from *In My Room: Designing for and with Children* by Antonio F. Torrice and Ro Logrippo.)

Activities	Child 1	Child 2	Child 3
Age	——	——	——
arts and crafts	——	——	——
building blocks	——	——	——
board games	——	——	——
collections	——	——	——
(awards, trophies)	——	——	——
computer work	——	——	——
dance	——	——	——
dolls and stuffed animals	——	——	——
exercise	——	——	——
fantasy play	——	——	——
living things	——	——	——
(pets and plants; what kinds?)	——	——	——
music	——	——	——
(what instruments?)	——	——	——
personal grooming	——	——	——
puppet theater	——	——	——
puzzles	——	——	——
reading	——	——	——
science experiments	——	——	——
stamp and coin collecting	——	——	——
telephone conversations	——	——	——
video and television	——	——	——
other: _____	——	——	——
other: _____	——	——	——
other: _____	——	——	——
other: _____	——	——	——

18.   How do you prefer to light your children's bedrooms?

19.   Describe any other requirements for your children's bedrooms.

If your budget must be cut, what compromises are acceptable?

9

BATHROOMS

"When all else fails, bathe."

—Jody Bergsma

CHECKLIST

(No response is required. These are standard items that should not be overlooked.)

1. Are the bathrooms close to the bedrooms?

2. Is there at least a half-bath near the main living area?

3. If possible, is there an operable window in each bathroom in an accessible location?

4. Are bathroom fans on timer switches?

5. Do the bathtub and bathroom floors have slip-resistant finishes?

6. Have you allowed at least twenty-four inches of floor space in front of the toilet, lavatory, shower, and bathtub?

7. If possible, has the toilet been placed so it is not visible through an open door?

8. Is there a place to hang a towel and bathrobe not more than one foot from the shower?

9. Have you allowed a minimum of two feet of towel rack for each person using the bathroom?

10. Have you allowed a special storage space for each person using the bathroom?

11. Have you allowed space for laundry hampers and bathroom scales?

12. Are there ample electrical outlets located near the sink and mirror?

13. Is there a grab bar next to the bathtub? (Grab bars should be at least three-quarters of an inch in diameter, easy to grasp, slip-resistant, and capable of supporting a 300-pound static load.)

14. Does the bathtub have a comfortable contoured (slanted) surface that fits the body?

15. Are there grab bars in the shower? (Preferably, they should be located near the shower entry and inside the shower stall, approximately 40 inches high.)

16. Do hinged shower doors swing out?

17. Does each bathroom have a lighted switch plate for safety in the dark?

18. Have you allowed for a ceiling fixture above the mirror and a light on each side of the mirror, at eye level, so a face can be illuminated without shadows? (All three fixtures should be wired to and controlled by one switch.)

19. Have you chosen incandescent bulb lighting or full-spectrum flourescent lighting where makeup will be applied? (These types of illumination are closest to sunlight in color.)

20. Have you allowed ample, easily accessible space for a medicine cabinet?

21. Have you allowed for storage of cleaning supplies, toilet paper, and personal hygiene supplies in the bathroom? (A shallow wall cabinet installed above the toilet is convenient for personal hygiene supplies.)

EXERCISES

GENERAL CONSIDERATIONS

1. For each bathroom planned, describe who will be using the facilities (parents, children, guests) and how you visualize the space. Some of the following ideas may stimulate your thinking:

a view of the outdoors?
small and enclosed?
open and spacious?
shared or private?
single room or compartmentalized?
bright, sunny bath or cozy and softly lighted?
many decorative objects on view or tidy and uncluttered?

	Principal Users	Where Located	Qualities Desired
Master bath	_____	_____	_____
	_____	_____	_____
Bath #2	_____	_____	_____
	_____	_____	_____
Bath #3	_____	_____	_____
	_____	_____	_____

Most showers cannot be turned on without dousing one's hair in cold water or being scalded because water controls are improperly placed directly under the water source. Locating the water controls near the door prevents these problems. This shower area is 36 inches in width, 60 inches in length, with the shower spray (water source) on the shorter side (width). A seat or footrest is provided for washing feet or shaving legs. Note the storage shelf at standing height. Two 40-inch-high support bars should be located inside the shower stall and directly outside the shower area, where a person could slip when exiting.

CHILDREN'S BATHROOMS

2. Ideally, children should have their own bathrooms. Think of the fun you used to have playing in the bath and you will know how important it is to make a child's bathroom flooring slip-resistant and waterproof. Parents should provide a sturdy step stool to make it easier for children to reach the adult-height sink. Check the requirements below that are important to you:

___ lever-style door handles (easier to grasp)

___ a place for everything in easy reach of young children

___ bright, primary colors (If not, what colors do you prefer?)

_____

___ slip-resistant/waterproof flooring: What is your preference? Specially treated cork, linoleum, studded rubber tiles, or slip resistant tile are all viable, although ceramic tile is not the safest. (If you choose it, do not put breakable objects in your bathroom.)

Flooring: _____

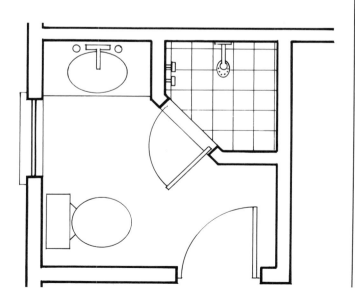

An efficient bathroom for a small space.

_____ lever-style faucets

_____ thermostatic-controlled faucets (protects shower and tub users against hot/cold surges; in 1991 prices, add $75)

IMPORTANCE OF BATHROOM FEATURES

3. For your bathrooms, rank on a 1 to 4 scale (1 = most important, 4 = least important) the following features:

	Master	Bath #2	Bath #3
tub/shower combined	_____	_____	_____
tub/shower separate	_____	_____	_____
bathtub only	_____	_____	_____
hand-held spray in bathtub	_____	_____	_____
shower only	_____	_____	_____
Jacuzzi	_____	_____	_____
one sink	_____	_____	_____
two sinks	_____	_____	_____
planter	_____	_____	_____
skylight	_____	_____	_____
sit-down makeup area	_____	_____	_____
oversized window	_____	_____	_____
"his and hers" drawers	_____	_____	_____
towel/linen storage	_____	_____	_____
private commode	_____	_____	_____
pedestal lavatory	_____	_____	_____
dressing area	_____	_____	_____
magazine/book rack	_____	_____	_____
bath-toy storage	_____	_____	_____

overhead heat lamp   _____   _____   _____

auxiliary heat source (a nice
    touch if you keep your
    house thermostat low)   _____   _____   _____

standard toilet   _____   _____   _____

elongated toilet (offers 1½ to 2
    inches of additional seating
    room, provides more com-
    fort, costs a little more)   _____   _____   _____

GUESTS

4. Will you require a separate powder room for guests (with a toilet and sink)?

5. Will guests use one of the family bathrooms? If so, which one?

SPECIAL REQUIREMENTS

6. Do you want to compartmentalize any of your bathrooms by separating the tub, shower, and toilet (which will need a fan) from the sink area? (This is convenient for children of opposite sexes sharing the same bathroom.)

Many families can avoid the additional expense of a separate powder room by combining it with an existing bathroom.

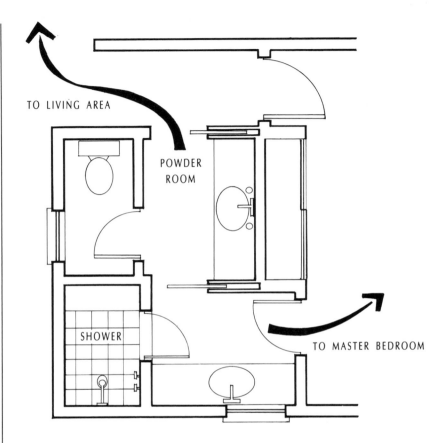

TO LIVING AREA

POWDER ROOM

SHOWER

TO MASTER BEDROOM

7. Will you have unusual storage needs in your bathroom, such as for exercise equipment?

8. Will any of the bathrooms be used for other than normal bathroom purposes? (For example, will any of the bathrooms include an exercise area, a laundry area, a sauna, or serve as an added place to relax, or an extension of the master suite?)

9. Do you have special requirements for any of your bathrooms, such as a diaper-changing area, extra grab bars for the elderly, or a sink large enough for shampooing hair?

10. Do you prefer separate "his and hers" vanities in your master bath versus one long two-person vanity? (Consider the drawback of the added width of two sinks and two faucets versus how many minutes per day two people may need to use the same sink. As an alternative to two vanities, you might prefer to invest in one nice sink and a special faucet.)

11. The standard height of a vanity and basin is thirty-four inches. Will you want them to be

    _____ higher than standard?
    _____ lower than standard?

12. Do you read in the bathtub? (If so, plan adequate lighting and a place to put books or magazines.)

13. Do special requests for your tub include:

    _____ sunken? (*Note: Accidents have occurred when people have fallen into a sunken tub in the dark.*)
    _____ set in a raised platform? (*Note: A bathtub installed in a raised platform may be awkward to climb in and out of. Install a grab bar and slip-resistant steps to assist with the climb.*)

_____ tucked into an alcove?

_____ other? _____

14. Do you want opaque or clear glass in your master bath shower stall?

15. Do you have special requirements for shower head heights?

16. Do you want a personal shower (detachable or adjustable vertically) in any of your bathrooms? (This can be handy for bathing animals, young children, or for use by those with disabilities.)

A separate makeup area (shown at right, between the sink and shower stall) includes a lowered counter, special lighting, a mirror, storage, and comfortable seating. Another built-in convenience is the seating area adjoining the raised tub.

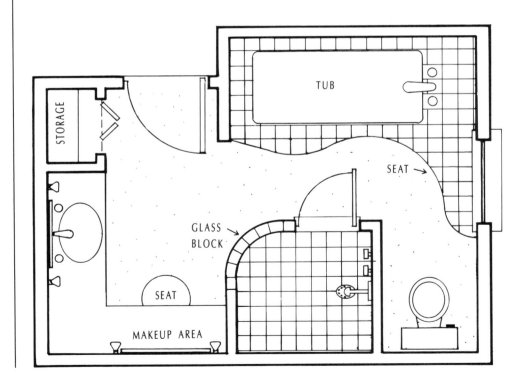

LIGHTING

17. How do you prefer to light your bathrooms? (A diffused light is easier on the eyes than a harsh direct light. Dimmer switches are recommended for bathrooms. Other lighting concerns have been covered previously in the bathroom checklist section.)

18. Do you put on makeup without glasses or contacts, therefore needing a well-lit mirror that offers close-in accessibility? (See the illustration opposite for an example of a separate makeup area within a bathroom.)

19. Additional thoughts:

If your budget must be cut, what compromises are acceptable?

10

LAUNDRY AREA

"After ecstasy, the laundry."

—Unknown

. . . .

THE LAUNDRY ROOM

The laundry room can be as simple as two machines in a closet or as ornate as a multi-purpose utility/hobby room with built-ins for various activities.

Many homes have the messy practicalities of everyday life stuffed into an array of closets or oozing into the living areas or kitchen. Consider grouping some of these objects into a utilitarian, practical laundry area storage.

Consider also whether you want your laundry room to serve as a hobby workshop space, using the existing countertops for wrapping presents, arranging flowers, sewing, art projects, or model making.

Often, families with children and animals like to use the laundry room as a back door foyer or mudroom to keep some of the mess from making its way into the house. See the illustration on page 142.

CHECKLIST
(No response is required. These are standard items that should not be overlooked.)

1. Is a high-level cupboard, out of the reach of young children, available for storing washing powders, bleaches, stain removers, and so forth?

2. Have provisions been made for accidental washer overflow? (For example, a floor drain or a washing tray with a drain.)

3. Is the clothes dryer located near an outside framed wall for ease of venting?

EXERCISES

1. Where do you wish to locate your laundry?

   ——— close to kitchen
   ——— close to bedrooms
   ——— close to basement
   ——— close to outdoors

2. Do you do your own laundry? Your own sewing? If you do both, do you want to combine these rooms?

3. Check the items that you will require in your laundry:

   ——— washer   brand: ——————————   color: ——————————
   ——— dryer   brand: ——————————   color: ——————————
   ——— sink
   ——— fold-down ironing board*
   ——— storage cupboards
   ——— clothes sorting bins
   ——— a separate bin for clothes to take to the cleaners
   ——— counter space for folding clothes
   ——— clothing rod for hanging clothes
   ——— drying rack (for hang-drying clothes)
   ——— laundry chute (for houses with more than one story)

*If you will not be ironing in your laundry area, where do you want to locate your ironing board?

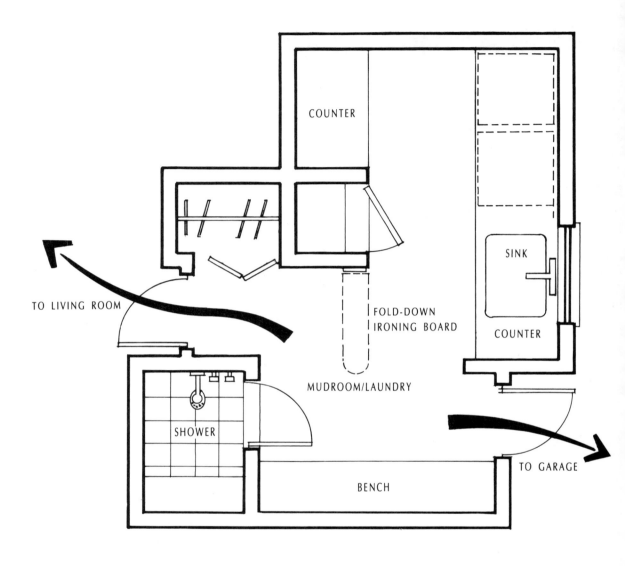

COUNTER

SINK

COUNTER

TO LIVING ROOM

FOLD-DOWN
IRONING BOARD

MUDROOM/LAUNDRY

SHOWER

BENCH

TO GARAGE

Mudroom/laundry. Cleaning up after outside work or play is easy with a shower in the mudroom/ laundry. Note the bench conveniently placed near the shower to assist in removing muddy clothes.

4. Check the other items you want to locate in your laundry:

——— storage for wrapping paper and ribbons

——— storage for animal food, kitty litter, leashes, and animal bathing supplies

——— cleaning supplies

——— chemicals and poisons

——— shoe care supplies

——— coat hooks

——— a boot shelf

——— vases and flower arranging materials

——— tools for minor repairs

——— art and craft supplies

——— specialty small sports equipment (such as ski goggles, gloves, knapsacks, water bottles)

——— camping equipment that should be stored indoors (such as down-filled sleeping bags and tents)

——— an emergency supply box

5. If possible, do you want a window in your laundry?

6. Do you wish to have the laundry room function as a mudroom?

If your budget must be cut, what compromises are acceptable?

11

ADDITIONAL ROOMS AND SPACES

"Think about your design as if it were poetry. Architecture as an art form gives each of us the possibility of life filled with meaning. . . . The houses we design will most likely exist after we are gone, leaving a record of our dreams for coming generations."

—Dennis Holloway and Maureen McIntyre,
The Owner-Builder Experience

EXERCISES

OFFICE

1. Do you want an office at home? If so, describe the office equipment you now own or plan to purchase, and your countertop, filing, and storage needs.

HOBBIES AND OTHER SPECIAL NEEDS

2. Do any family members have particular hobbies? If so, describe. Will a special room or alcove be needed to accommodate a major hobby? If so, elaborate.

3. Will any other special rooms be required?
    ____ recreation room
    ____ den/library
    ____ studio
    ____ workshop

Built-in bookshelves and a laminated wood spiral staircase provide warmth and elegance and turn this corner of a ''great space'' into a library.

4. Do you own or plan to own a home video entertainment system?

   If so, where would you like this located?

5. Do you own or anticipate owning a computer system?

   If so, where would you like this located?

6. Do you want to allocate space for a home gym? Describe where you would like to locate it and the equipment it will contain (weights, exercise bike, slant board, mini trampoline, and so on).

BASEMENT

7. Do you plan to have a full or partial basement? (In climates where frost penetration requires deep footings, basements are often desirable and can house mechanical equipment economically. In localities where weather conditions are more temperate and deep foundation walls are not required, or where the water table is high, basements are often undesirable.)

8. If you want a basement, what specific functions will it serve? (Ideas: recreation room, office, den, workshop, sleeping space, self-contained apartment, storage area, laundry area, music practice.)

GARAGE / CARPORT AND LAYING OUT A DRIVEWAY

9. What size garage or carport will you require?

_____ two-car

_____ two-and-a-half-car

_____ three-car

(See page 150 for driveway layout considerations. If you don't have space for the recommendations there, before installing your driveway, mark your driveway boundaries with stakes and string, and practice various entry and exit maneuvers until you're satisfied you've allotted adequate space.)

10. If you want a two-car garage, have you considered a two-and-a-half or three-car garage for additional low-cost storage or shop space?

11. Do you want a window in your garage? (If security is a problem in your area, we recommend opaque glass.)

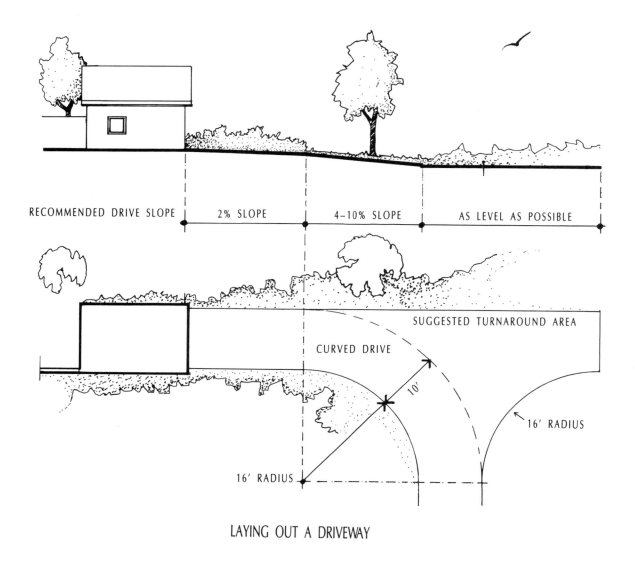

RECOMMENDED DRIVE SLOPE | 2% SLOPE | 4–10% SLOPE | AS LEVEL AS POSSIBLE

SUGGESTED TURNAROUND AREA

CURVED DRIVE

10'

16' RADIUS

16' RADIUS

LAYING OUT A DRIVEWAY

The top drawing illustrates minimum and maximum slope considerations to prevent bottoming out. It also promotes good drainage. The lower drawing shows minimum turning radius requirements. If you require a turnaround, make it eighteen feet in length and at least ten feet wide to allow turnaround room for delivery trucks. If you live in a snowy winter climate, you should increase these recommended distances.

12. Do you want an automatic garage door opener?

13. Do you own a boat, trailer, RV, or motorcycle that you want to store in the garage or elsewhere on your property?

14. Will you have any special requirements regarding electrical outlets in your garage for shop equipment?

If your budget must be cut, what compromises are acceptable?

STORAGE AREAS AND CLOSETS

"Clutter increases the friction in your life. It takes more energy to operate your home, your office, or your relationships."

—Bottom Line Newsletter

. . . .

CHECKLIST

(No response is required. These are standard items that should not be overlooked.)

1. Have you allowed for the following closet space? (See the first illustration on page 157 for an excellent way to allow for storage under a pitched roof.)

    _____ hall or coat closet (near entry, with adequate space for guest use)

    _____ utility closet

    _____ linen closet

    _____ closets for each bedroom

    _____ basement/attic storage

    _____ bathroom cabinet

    _____ kitchenware and food storage cabinets

2. Are built-in drawers on guides?

EXERCISES

GENERAL CONSIDERATIONS

1. Do you want closet organization systems in any of your bedroom closets? If so, which ones?

2. Do you want your master bedroom closet to be part of a bathing/ dressing suite?

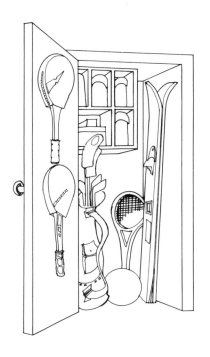

3. Do you want a large walk-in closet in your master bedroom area? Do you store some clothes in dressers, chests, and other furniture, or will all of your clothes and accessories be stored in the closet?

4. Do you want any of your closets to function with a "door button" light so that the light is activated only when the door is opened? (This is a nice feature for a hall or coat closet, or any closet located in a dark area.)

   If so, which closets?

CUSTOMIZED BUILT-INS

5. Rank on a 1 to 4 scale the additional built-in storage you will require (1 = most important, 4 = least important). Refer to the illustrations on pages 155 and 157 for storage ideas.

_____ living room closet	_____ stereo system
_____ pantry	_____ records/CDs/tapes
_____ china and tableware	_____ extra bedding
_____ sports equipment	_____ VCR/video storage
_____ wine storage	_____ photography equipment
_____ root cellar	_____ animal food/dishes
_____ canned, preserved goods	_____ mail/bills
_____ card table and extension leaf	_____ bookshelves
_____ tools	_____ hobby closet
_____ fireplace wood	_____ garden furniture
_____ music books and equipment	_____ garden tools, hoses, etc.
_____ games and toys	_____ trunks and suitcases
_____ children's outdoor toys	_____ holiday celebration materials
_____ playpen, highchair	_____ wrapping paper, boxes, and ribbons*
_____ out-of-season clothes	_____ other: _____
_____ screens and screen doors	_____

*Do you want a pull-out bin drawer for long rolls of wrapping paper? If so, where?

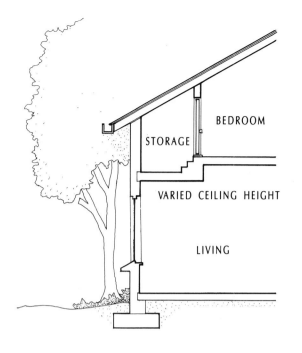

STORAGE

BEDROOM

VARIED CEILING HEIGHT

LIVING

Storage space can be provided in low window-less areas under a pitched roof. Dropping the floor level in the storage to allow adequate headroom provides ceiling height variation in the level below. (Long-term storage spaces must be well-sealed to prevent pests and insulated—include a vapor barrier—to prevent mildew.)

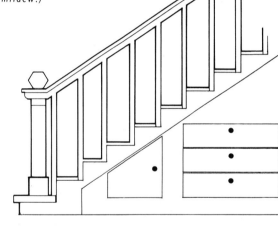

Valuable storage space can often be located under stairs.

If your budget must be cut, what compromises are acceptable?

13

OUTSIDE SPACES

"Somewhere in every garden, there must be at least one spot, a quiet garden seat, in which a person—or two people—can reach into themselves and be in touch with nothing else but nature."

—Christopher Alexander et al.,
A Pattern Language

· ·

CHECKLIST

(No response is required. These are standard items that should not be overlooked.)

1. Can the entry be easily located by first-time visitors?

2. Has room been allowed for visitor parking?

3. Is the house number prominent?

4. Are porches and balconies at least six feet deep? (Anything less is unlikely to be used.)

5. Are features such as plumbing vents, gutter downspouts, and furnace vents carefully located to prevent unsightliness?

6. Can windows be easily reached for washing?

7. Is the house safe from damage from falling trees or tree branches?

8. Can tree droppings (sap, leaves, needles) be easily cleaned from roof and gutters?

9. Is the exterior lighting adequate to provide safe nighttime access and egress?

10. Is exterior lighting sufficient to discourage vandalism?

11. Is the yard relatively safe for children?

12. Are decks safe enough for a crawling baby?

13. Are pools and hot tubs situated so as to prevent accidental drownings?

14. Is water for firefighting available so that a hose can reach any part of the site should a fire break out?

15. Is there easy access for the meter reader?

16. Are septic tanks and oil or propane tanks easily accessible for service without damage to the landscaping?

17. Does stored refuse have a barrier to prevent bacteria and smells from polluting the outside air? Is such storage out of sight?

18. Is refuse for collection stored in such a way as to facilitate ease of transfer to a disposal unit?

19. Are all entries to the house well protected with a generous porch or overhang?

EXERCISES

1. What feeling do you want to create in your home's outside area?

2. What is most important to you about landscaping and outdoor living?

3. From other outside spaces you have visited, what have you seen that most appeals to you?

4. Rank on a 1 to 4 scale the importance of the following indoor/outdoor features (1 = most important, 4 = least important):

	Rank	Location
covered porch	____	_____
screened porch	____	_____
covered deck	____	_____
open deck	____	_____
covered patio	____	_____
open patio	____	_____

5. If you enjoy outdoor dining, what facilities do you want?

    ____ a covered barbecue area

    ____ a serving counter

    ____ a serving bar (pass-through from the kitchen)

    ____ space for table and chairs

    ____ other: _____

    Describe the atmosphere you would like to create.

6. Some families want a bonfire or fire circle in their backyard as an enjoyable way for family and friends to gather and talk on a cool

night. If you want this option, how would it work best in the back-yard you envision?

_____ a separate bonfire area
Will the seating be permanent? _____

_____ part of a barbecue pit

_____ a stone-encircled firepit

7. Think back to your favorite outside childhood spaces. How were these spaces defined (landscaping, fences, trees, hedges, walkways, hiding places)?

8. Why did you like these outdoor spaces?

9. What did you like to do in these spaces?

10. What smells and sounds can you remember?

11. What was the impact of weather on these spaces?

12. How did you feel in these spaces?

13. What houses of friends and relatives did you enjoy visiting?

   What was special about their entries or outside spaces?

TERRACES

In northern climates, during the warm months of the year, a terrace can become an outdoor living room. The terrace should be located adjacent to the home with one or more rooms opening onto it, and should offer privacy and a balanced amount of sunlight and shade. The goal is to make

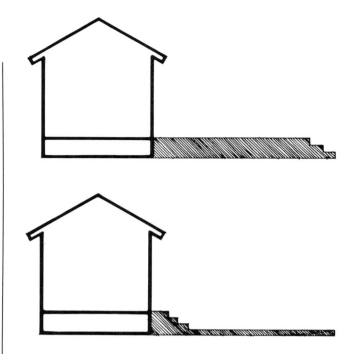

the terrace feel like an extension of the home. The most important principle
is to elevate your terrace so it is as close to the level of your home as
possible. This will offer an intimate connection between house and terrace.
(See above.) Also, if the only possible location for your terrace is on the
west side of your home, you will need to plant shade trees a short distance
to the west of the terrace because the western sun comes in at a near-
horizontal angle.

14. A southwest orientation will create the warmest exterior areas; a
     northeast corner will create the coolest. Do you want to use different
     areas in different seasons? Which rooms do you want to have access
     to outside areas?

15. Do you want to provide a place for special outdoor furniture, hammocks, or porch swings?

16. Do you want to provide areas for children's play (sandbox, wading pool, playhouse, swing set)?

Is it important that these be viewed from specific rooms?

If so, which ones?

WALKWAYS

Walkways are frequently the most overlooked area of outside planning. When your home is under construction, and before your step and walkway options become set in brick, stone, or concrete, spend some of your many hours at your construction site wandering your grounds. Consider the various visual and practical connections that will bring unity to your landscape plan. How do you think your family will best use your outside spaces? If you have dogs, bring them to your site and observe the pathways they create so you'll know not to locate unprotected flower beds in those places! (Refer to the important information in the following pages on designing outdoor steps.)

17. What general observations do you have at this point concerning your home's exterior walkways and steps?

OUTDOOR STEP DIMENSION RECOMMENDATIONS

No dimension of landscape planning is so frequently overlooked as is the planning of outdoor steps. A surprising number of builders, as well as most homeowners, are not familiar with the principles that should govern the design of a flight of steps. The following has been excerpted from *Betty Ajay's Guide to Home Landscaping:*

TREAD-RISER RELATIONSHIPS

The safety of a flight of steps is not determined by any specific width of tread or height of riser, as many people think, but by the relationship between the two. This relationship is governed by the length of a stride. A person of average height should be able to go up or down a flight of steps without shortening or lengthening his normal stride. This means that a high riser requires a narrow tread and a lower riser requires a broader tread. A useful formula for determining the correct relationship between the tread and riser is: *twice the riser plus the tread should equal twenty-six.* The following correct tread-riser relationships are based on this formula:

8″ riser—10″ tread	5″ riser—16″ tread
7″ riser—12″ tread	4″ riser—18″ tread
6″ riser—14″ tread	3″ riser—20″ tread

These relationships can be varied, but only slightly, if steps are to be safe and comfortable.

STEPS FROM HOUSE TO LAND

When there is no porch or terrace, steps leading from the house should begin with a platform immediately outside the threshold. This platform should be deep enough so that someone standing on it can pull open the screen or storm door without having to step back off the platform. (The minimum depth would be four feet.)

In the majority of houses built without an architect, the steps leading from the house are planned by the builder without the participation of the owner. The average builder knows that indoor steps usually have a ten-inch or twelve-inch tread with a riser of eight inches or seven inches. He also knows that if he varies the tread without changing the riser, or vice versa, the steps will be hazardous. When he builds his outdoor steps, therefore, he most often uses the same tread-riser relationship that he has always used indoors. This produces steps that are safe but improperly scaled for most exteriors. The typical flight of outdoor steps planned by a builder has high risers and narrow treads and is, consequently, steep and precipitous. It bridges the two levels in the shortest amount of space with the hardest climbing. Steps with low risers and broad treads take up more space, provide a more gentle transition between levels, and tie the house more effectively to its surroundings.

The most suitable tread-riser relationship will vary, but in most cases where there is a small change in elevation, the broadest tread and lowest riser that can be worked into the specific situation are the best choice. To arrive at the most suitable dimensions for a particular flight of steps, the distance between the threshold and the finished grade is the dimension that is used to figure the various possibilities. (There is always one less tread than there are risers, since the last riser brings you to level ground which is, in effect, a tread.) If the threshold of the house is sixteen inches above grade and a forty-eight-inch platform is used, the alternatives would be as follows:

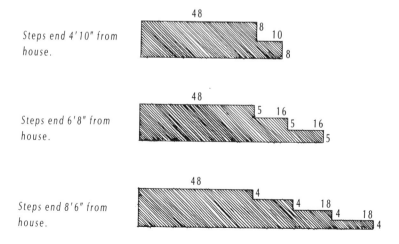

Steps end 4'10" from house.

Steps end 6'8" from house.

Steps end 8'6" from house.

Using stakes and string, the steps should be staked out in each of the alternate ways. If the house is large and there is ample space, the eighteen-inch tread and four-inch riser will usually make the most attractive step, but if the house is small or space is limited, this tread-riser relationship will not be practical because the steps will be too broad and will occupy too much space. The sixteen-inch tread and five-inch riser would then be the next choice. The last alternative, a tread of ten inches with an eight-inch riser, should never be used on steps leading from a house unless broader treads and lower risers just will not fit into the available space.

Steps leading from the house should be wide as well as broad. A width that would be appropriate indoors looks far too narrow when it is seen in relation to the expanse of an entire house.

Many houses with well-designed front steps have side and back steps that are poorly designed, even though these areas are often the only ones in which the family has any privacy, and consequently are the ones most frequently used. As much care should be spent in designing the steps leading from the secondary doors as is spent in designing the steps leading from the front door, and materials of comparable quality should be used.

OTHER LANDSCAPING NEEDS

18. Do you want an in-ground sprinkler system?

19. Do you want a protected work space for potting and transplanting?

20. Do you want an herb garden or vegetable garden with easy access to your kitchen?

21. If you compost, where do you want your compost pile?

22. Do you want the exterior lighting designed for a variety of light levels—floodlights at all exterior corners for occasional use and more subtle lighting for everyday use?

Do you want to create dramatic accents with uplighting or down-lighting, such as featuring a special tree?

If so, where?

23. Do you want to install low-voltage lighting? (An excellent alternative to standard outdoor lighting, it uses less energy, is cheaper to operate, and is very easy to install.)

24. Do you want to light a deck or patio? (If so, perimeter lighting is one of the most effective ways. Position the lamps to spread light on shrubs and flowers, with less intense light on the deck or patio area.)

25. Do you want to activate any outside lights with a photocell switch so that lights will come on at dusk and turn off at dawn?

26. What other thoughts, ideas, or feelings do you have concerning your outdoor space?

If your budget must be cut, what compromises are acceptable?

WHAT'S IN A NAME?

Legally and conceptually there are differences between a garden designer, landscape designer, landscape architect, and landscape contractor. A garden designer or landscape designer can be anyone who designs outdoor spaces—even a homeowner who scribbles out ideas on scraps of paper and hands them over to others to implement. Whether a person is called a *garden* designer or a *landscape* designer is often a matter of semantics, though garden designers tend to place a greater emphasis on plants, while landscape designers work more with durable materials such as redwood, brick, paving, and gravel.

Landscape architects must be licensed by the state or province. To qualify as a landscape architect in the state of California, for example, requires at least three years of training under a landscape architect, a four-year degree, and the passing of both written and oral examinations covering the legalities and history of landscape architecture, design, construction, and plant materials.

A landscape contractor, on the other hand, is the state-licensed person who physically moves the earth and does the construction—like a building contractor. This is the person with the bulldozer, the backhoe, and the labor to transform blueprints executed by a landscape architect into beautiful vistas, contoured berms, stone terraces, and other design elements.

—Elizabeth Murray and Derek Fell,
Home Landscaping

14

OTHER CONSIDERATIONS

*"Design your home with love
as it will house
the voices of your future."*

—*Steve Myrvang*

CHECKLIST

(No response is required. These are standard items that should not be overlooked.)

1. Does your existing or planned-for furniture fit the floor plan? (Go through the house plan room by room.)

2. Are hallways where doors/drawers open into them at least three and a half feet wide? (This prevents unnecessary people congestion.)

3. Does each room have adequate lighting with a switch immediately inside the door? (For a room with a separate egress, install a two-way switch.)

4. Are appropriate light fixtures on dimmers?

5. Are switches installed at all stair locations, one at the top and one at the bottom?

6. Are smoke alarms in the proper locations to ensure safety: tops of stairs, near kitchen, bedroom hallways?

7. Are multiple fire-escape routes planned from every room and floor in your home?

8. Are forced-air heater vents placed away from furniture and major floor plants?

9. For colder climates, is a drain-down valve provided where standing water in pipes may freeze?

EXERCISES

DOORS, LOCKS, SYSTEMS, AND MORE

1. For closing off individual rooms, do you prefer to use pocket, or sliding, doors?

   ___ as much as possible?

   ___ moderately (such as between a master bedroom and bath, or for a pantry)?

   ___ only where a regular door takes up too much floor space for a given area?

2. Which interior doors will require locks?

3. Will you require extra-wide halls and stairways to accommodate any large, bulky items you own? If yes, describe.

4. Which rooms or areas will require phone jacks?

   Do you own a cordless phone or an answering device? (If so, install a duplex outlet with those phone jacks.)

5. Do you want an intercom system?

6. Do you want a central vacuum system?

7. Do you want a centralized electronic control system (often referred to as a "smart home")?

8. If not, would you prefer to have a few lights electronically controlled? If so, which ones? (This is inexpensive.)

9. Do you want a recirculating hot water system to eliminate excessive waiting for hot water at plumbing fixtures?

10. Do you want a hot tub or sauna? If so, where?

11. What type of security system will you require? Check all that apply.

　　_____ dead bolt on exterior doors

　　_____ outdoor lighting such as a low-voltage system that turns on automatically at dusk

_____ motion-sensing light switch to discourage potential intruders

_____ burglar alarm system. It is often economical to install a fire alarm system along with your burglar alarm system. Do you want both? _____

_____ other: _____

(Read the excellent book *The Complete Guide to Home Security*, listed in the bibliography, page 233.)

12. Do you want a fire sprinkler system? (For a new house of 2,000 square feet, the 1992 installed cost may range from $1,500 to $3,000. Refer to Table 1, page 215.)

13. Do you want to use glass block in your home? (Glass block is an attractive way to screen undesirable outside views or to provide privacy while admitting light. One can use a few glass blocks judiciously to create a desired effect, but an entire wall of glass blocks can be expensive. See page 11 for an example of a relatively inexpensive application.)

GUESTS

14. How will you accommodate overnight guests in your home? (Keep bathroom access and privacy in mind.)

15. Does anyone in your family, or do any frequent visitors, have difficulty climbing stairs?

DESIGNING FOR DISABILITY CONSIDERATIONS

Few people go through life without experiencing some kind of disability. Designing for the aged, the injured, and the handicapped involves special considerations for moving throughout the home, operating equipment or devices, and receiving maximum enjoyment from the home environment.

A well-insulated home is critical: The elderly and those with movement restriction are often sensitive to temperature variations. Zoned heating permits users to turn on heat in selected areas of the home.

Floor surfaces should be even and slip-resistant, especially in and around showers and tubs. Some vinyl and rubber products can provide an excellent floor surface for shower areas if properly sealed. High-pile carpets can hook shoe heels and should be avoided. Ceramic and quarry floor tiles, if uneven, may cause stumbling. Walls should be fairly smooth to decrease abrasions when catching oneself in a fall. If desired, computerized systems can turn on lights and control room temperature. Good task lighting will facilitate cooking, hobbying, and other close work. Light switches should be installed no higher than forty-eight inches from the floor to be accessible to the wheelchair user, and electrical outlets and telephone and television jacks should be eighteen inches, rather than the standard twelve inches, above the floor.

Safe passage between areas can be facilitated by eliminating level changes. Where stairs are required, make sure they have a tread length of eleven to twelve inches and a riser height six and a half to seven inches. Also, stairways with fewer than three risers may not be noticed by individuals with poor eyesight, which might result in a serious injury. Strong lighting is essential for illuminating stairs. Where the floor area allows, a ramp with a 1:12 slope and a sturdy handrail is a much safer transition between levels.

For wheelchair passage, doors need to be a minimum width of thirty-six inches and halls a minimum of forty-four inches. Also, a five-foot turning radius is needed for wheelchairs. Consider installing power-operated electric doors.

If a two-story home is desired, locate the kitchen, living room, and a bedroom and bathroom on the first level so an individual could perform all living, eating, sleeping, cleaning, and elimination functions on one level. For the bathroom, provide grab bars around the toilet, tub, and shower. In the shower, install a bench or corner seat so that users can safely sit while showering. New toilets are available that assist rising from the toilet, reducing stress on the hip joints.

All appliances should be installed at a convenient height for the disabled person; for example, a dryer could be placed on a platform for easier access. Appliance knobs are difficult for some; front-mounted touch-sensitive controls are preferred. Lever-style door handles and lever-operated mechanisms are recommended for those people suffering from arthritis.

Magnetic induction stove burners are a good choice for absentminded individuals because the stove burners stay cool if left on, decreasing the chance of burns or a fire.

Motion detectors and voice activation systems offer high-tech methods of operating electrical equipment: Lights turn off automatically by voice command or when movement is undetected.

Windowsills installed lower than twenty-four inches off the floor provide increased viewing for wheelchair-bound or bedridden individuals.

Many of these suggestions will also be helpful to those without a disability. The concept of "universal design" (designing houses and appliances to fit as many people as possible) is increasing in popularity. An open floor plan, wide doorways, easy-to-open cabinets, and all or most of a living space on the first floor will provide a functional home for a lifetime.

For a free thirty-six page booklet, *The Do-Able, Renewable Home*, write to the American Association of Retired Persons (AARP), Consumer Affairs Section, 601 E Street, N.W., Washington, D.C., or call (202) 434-2277.

16. If you plan to live in your home for a number of years, will you need to design your home for any disability considerations?

WINDOW CHOICES

Choosing the type of windows for your home is not always simple. You should select windows that:

- complement the style of your home
- adapt to your home's framing system
- are weathertight and energy-efficient
- provide adequate daylight and ventilation
- are simple to operate and easy to clean
- are inexpensive to maintain
- provide a means of escape in case of a fire

You will undoubtedly be faced with trade-offs. For example, a fixed window is more energy-efficient than an operable window, but offers no ventilation or escape route. You may also want to consider investing in the new types of window glass, which are coated with a material that allows sunlight to enter the home, yet inhibits heat from radiating back outside. Tinted, reflective window films are another option for warm climates, reflecting both heat and light yet allowing a view to the outside.

17. Are there specific rooms where you would like to have one or more skylights? If so, where? (Many people like skylights for dramatic

effect—for example, near the entry or in the kitchen. For practical purposes, they should be used in any important room that has little natural light, such as from only one exterior window. Many skylights are operable and have black-out shades and screens.)

18. Are there specific rooms where you would like stained-glass or beveled-glass windows? If so, where? (For stained glass, an entry door side panel is a common use. Also, stained glass is an attractive way to screen undesirable outside views, or to provide privacy. Beveled glass is best used for windows with lots of sunlight. The sun on the beveling produces delightful prisms of light throughout the room. Both of these options are expensive compared to normal window glass.)

19. Do you want to use interior windows in your home, where feasible, to provide additional natural light and/or viewing?

WINDOW FRAMES AND COVERINGS

Wood is a natural insulator. Moisture does not condense on it as readily as on uninsulated metal. The disadvantage is that wood requires more maintenance than metal or vinyl and is usually more expensive.

Metal frames are stronger than wood. Aluminum is the most common metal used in residences, although steel finished with an antirust treatment and a coat of paint is also used.

Vinyl frames are not as stiff as wood or metal. They never require painting and come in a variety of colors.

Vinyl-clad wood frames offer a low maintenance vinyl exterior and a wood finished interior.

An awning window is similar to a casement, except that the former is hinged at the top rather than the side. Awning windows provide more ventilation than double-hung or sliding windows, but less than casements because they do not open all the way out. A benefit is that awning windows usually keep out rain even when open.

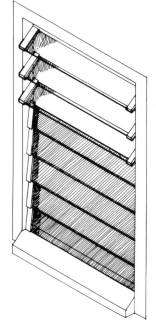

A jalousie window is composed of narrow horizontal slats that are held in place at the sides; they operate like a group of small awning windows. Jalousie windows are popular in hot tropical climes for maximal ventilation, but do not close tightly and allow too much air infiltration in colder regions.

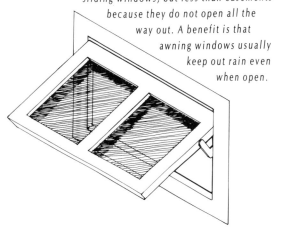

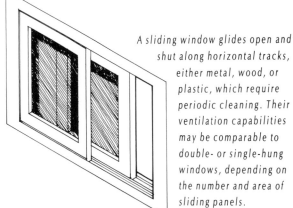

A sliding window glides open and shut along horizontal tracks, either metal, wood, or plastic, which require periodic cleaning. Their ventilation capabilities may be comparable to double- or single-hung windows, depending on the number and area of sliding panels.

A casement window is hinged at the side to swing outward and open by means of a crank or lever. Casements provide maximum ventilation and are easy to clean. To obtain maximum ventilation, make sure to specify that both sides of a double casement be operable and verify the degrees of opening both for ventilation and for egress. One note of caution: Do not locate casement windows where they could conflict with outside pedestrian traffic.

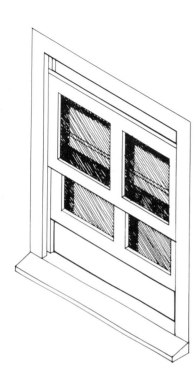

A double-hung window is one of the most popular window styles. It has two sashes that slide vertically. A double-hung window is not a good choice above a kitchen sink, a countertop, or a large piece of furniture, as there may not be sufficient leverage to open or close it easily.

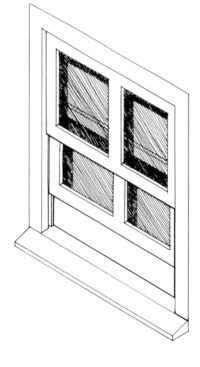

A single-hung window looks much the same as a double-hung window, but has only one moveable sash, usually the bottom one. A single-hung window usually costs less than a double-hung window. Because its upper section is fixed, a single-hung window will be more energy-efficient. The trade-off is that a single-hung window offers less ventilation flexibility.

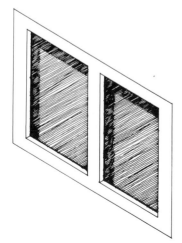

A fixed window does not open; it is used primarily for view, decorative effect, and passive solar heating.

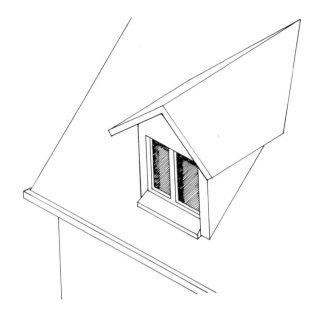

20. What is your preference for window frame materials and types?

21. What types of window coverings do you want? (Ideas: drapes, Roman shades, venetian blinds, vertical louver blinds, shutters. The types of window treatments desired may help determine the type of windows selected. For example, drapes look best on long, vertical windows. For some windows, you may want a dual-treatment: for example, venetian blinds for light control and Roman shades for softness.)

Room or Area   Window Covering(s)

_____   _____

_____   _____

_____   _____

_____   _____

22. Use the space below to list anything that may have been overlooked.

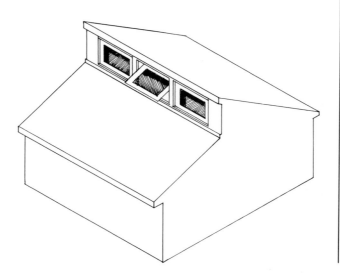

A clerestory window is located high on vertical walls to gather light, while usually offering privacy. Most clerestory windows are fixed, but can be installed with moveable sashes.

15

FINISHES AND FIXTURES

"God is in the detail."

—*Ludwig Mies van der Rohe*

Most people do not make a final choice of finishes until shortly before they begin to build, so do not feel overwhelmed with the information required in this chapter. If you know what you want in certain areas, complete those sections alone and fill in the rest as you get ideas.

Before turning the handbook over to your design professional for the design phase, you may want to duplicate this section so you can continue to record your selections in a leisurely manner as you research and shop for finishes.

EXTERIOR FINISH SCHEDULE

Siding _____   Stain / Paint Color _____

                                                Brand _____

Trim _____   Stain / Paint Color _____

                                                Brand _____

Doors _____   Stain / Paint Color _____

                                                Brand _____

Roof Covering* _____   Color _____

                                                Brand _____

Windows _____

Decks _____

Walks _____

Fences _____

*If you plan to install a noncombustible roofing material, such as concrete tile or special kinds of asphalt, check with your insurance agent to confirm that the roofing material qualifies for reduced fire insurance rates. (If you do choose a heavier roofing material such as concrete tile, make sure the structural frame can support the extra load.)

FLOOR COVERING MATERIALS

	Type	Brand	Style #	Color
Entry				
Living room				
Family room				
Kitchen				
Dining area				
Laundry area				
Upstairs hall				
Stairs				
Downstairs hall				
Master bathroom				
Bathroom #2				
Bathroom #3				
Master bedroom				
Dressing area				
Bedroom #2				
Bedroom #3				
Bedroom #4				
Special-purpose room				
Basement				

INTERIOR FINISH SCHEDULE FOR WALLS AND CEILINGS

	Paint Color	Trim Color	Wallpaper	Paneling	Tile
Entry					
Living room					
Family room					
Kitchen					
Dining area					
Laundry area					
Upstairs hall					
Stairs					
Downstairs hall					
Master bathroom					
Bathroom #2					
Bathroom #3					
Master bedroom					
Dressing area					
Bedroom #2					
Bedroom #3					
Bedroom #4					
Special-purpose room					
Garage					
Basement					

PLUMBING FIXTURES, FITTINGS, AND ACCESSORIES

		Fixture	Brand	Model #	Color
Kitchen	Sink(s)				
Serving bar	Sink				
Laundry	Sink				
Master bathroom	Basin(s)				
	Toilet				
	Bidet				
	Bathtub w/shower				
	Separate shower				
	Medicine cabinet(s)				
Bathroom #2	Basin(s)				
	Toilet				
	Bathtub w/shower				
	Separate shower				
	Medicine cabinet(s)				
Bathroom #3	Basin(s)				
	Toilet				
	Shower				
	Medicine cabinet(s)				

COUNTERTOPS

Some common choices, from least expensive to most expensive, are: plastic laminate, butcher block, ceramic tile, Corian®, granite, and marble. You may want a second or third material in your kitchen: for example, plastic laminate on most areas, ceramic tile inset next to the cooktop, and butcher block next to the sink or cooktop.

	Type	Brand	Style #	Color
Kitchen				
Laundry area				
Master bathroom				
Bathroom #2				
Bathroom #3				
Other:				
Other:				
Other:				
Other:				

ELECTRIC LIGHT FIXTURES

Interior Lighting

	Fixture	Brand	Model #	Color	Qty.	On Dimmer
Inside entry						
Living room						
Family room						
Kitchen						
Dining area						
Laundry area						
Upstairs hall						
Stairs						
Downstairs hall						
Master bathroom						
Bathroom #2						
Bathroom #3						
Master bedroom						
Dressing area						
Bedroom #2						
Bedroom #3						
Bedroom #4						

	Fixture	Brand	Model #	Color	Qty.	On Dimmer
Special-purpose room						
Garage						
Basement						
Other						
Other						
Other						
Other						

Exterior Lighting

	Fixture	Brand	Model #	Color	Qty.	On Photocell
Front entry						
Back entry						
Side entry						
Side entry						
Other						
Other						
Other						
Other						

Landscape Lighting

	Fixture	Brand	Model #	Color	Qty.	On Photocell
Front area						
Back area						
Side area						
Side area						
Other						
Other						
Other						
Other						

If your budget must be cut, what compromises are acceptable for your finishes and fixtures?

16

GETTING IT DONE
ON BUDGET

"Budget wisely; spend most on the things that receive the most wear and you really want to last, the ones you will use constantly."

—Terence Conran,
New House Book

BUDGET WORKSHEETS

Overall Cost Calculations

1. What is the anticipated square footage of your project?

2. What is your anticipated cost per square foot?*
    A. Multiply the overall square footage by the cost per square foot:

    _____ × $_____ = $_____
       total sq. ft.   cost/sq. ft.   Subtotal A

    B. The following items are not included in the above figure and must
    be considered separately:

    Sales tax on above subtotal:**   _____

    Land costs (include escrow, survey, top-
    ographic map, and perc test costs):   _____

    Architectural Fees: _____

    Blueprints: _____

    Engineering Fees: _____

    Interior Design Fees: _____

    Landscape Design Fees: _____

    Landscape Materials and Installation:**   _____

    Building / Other Permit Fees:**   _____

*Check with several reputable builders in your area for the estimated cost per square foot given the size of your project and the features and finishes desired.

**May be included in contractor's bid. (Note: some states such as Oregon have no sales tax.)

Site Development (septic/sewer, water hookup or well, tree removal, road, driveway, site repairs, grading, importation of fill or topsoil, irrigation, drainage):** _____

Utility Costs (electricity, heat source, cable TV, telephone hookups): _____

Window Coverings:** _____

Upholstery for Built-ins:** _____

Loan or Appraisal Fees: _____

Construction Interest: _____

Contingency: _____

Subtotal of B Items: _____

TOTAL COST $_____ + $_____ = $_____
　　　　　　　　　(A)　　　　　　　　　(B)

ESTIMATED COST BREAKDOWN

Your contractor's bid will normally include the following items. Double-check your contractor's bid with this list to verify that important items haven't been overlooked.

Start Up _____

Temporary Electric Power _____

Portable Toilet _____

**May be included in contractor's bid. (Note: some states such as Oregon have no sales tax.)

Excavation and Grading　　　　　_____

Fill Dirt/Topsoil/Hauling　　　　　_____

Sewer/Septic　　　　　_____

Water Hookup/Well　　　　　_____

Road/Driveway　　　　　_____

Walks/Porches　　　　　_____

Garage Floor　　　　　_____

Demolition/Cleanup (Remodel)　　　　　_____

Footings and Foundations　　　　　_____

Drain Tile/Waterproofing　　　　　_____

Concrete Flatwork (Slabs)　　　　　_____

Masonry　　　　　_____

Framing Materials　　　　　_____

Framing Labor　　　　　_____

Roofing　　　　　_____

Gutters　　　　　_____

Rough Plumbing　　　　　_____

Rough Electrical　　　　　_____

Heat/Ventilation/Air-Conditioning　　　　　_____

Sheet Metal　　　　　_____

Skylights　　　　　_____

Windows　　　　　_____

Exterior Doors/Garage   _____

Interior Doors   _____

Soffits and Siding   _____

Insulation/Weatherstripping   _____

Stucco and Plaster   _____

Drywall   _____

Finish Carpentry   _____

Woodstove/Fireplace   _____

Paint Exterior   _____

Paint Interior   _____

Wallpaper   _____

Stairs   _____

Hardwood Flooring   _____

Carpeting   _____

Resilient Floor Coverings   _____

Ceramic Tile/Marble   _____

Plastic Laminate   _____

Hardware   _____

Equipment   _____

Deck   _____

Millwork/Cabinets   _____

Lighting Fixtures   _____

Plumbing Fixtures   _____

Bath Accessories   _____

Security System   _____

Appliances   _____

Finish Grading   _____

Fencing   _____

Automatic Sprinkler System   _____

Finish Concrete   _____

Cleanup/Trash Removal   _____

Landscaping   _____

Extras   _____

Extras   _____

Extras   _____

Subtotal   _____

Profit (_____%)   _____

Overhead (_____%)   _____

Total Before Taxes   _____

Sales Tax (_____%)   _____

TOTAL CONSTRUCTION COST   _____

WORKING WITH A DESIGN PROFESSIONAL

The best way to plan a house that makes the most of your site and your lifestyle is to hire an architect. Well-conceived, well-designed, and well-built projects will, in most cases, increase your property's or home's resale value.

Simple, straightforward tasks, such as adding a dormer or a bay, are jobs that you and a contractor can probably handle together.

For complicated interior and exterior changes, large additions, or an entirely new home, you should consider the services of an architect. When planning a new home, it is wise to meet with an architect prior to obtaining your site. Different sites have variable cost implications depending on the extent of site preparation needed. Many architects and house designers are willing to meet with you on an hourly basis, at your home or site, to discuss your project and offer suggestions. You need not commit yourself at this stage.

What is the difference between an architect and a designer? To become a licensed architect, one must usually complete a rigorous course of study at an accredited college or university, spend from three to eight years apprenticing with a licensed architect, and then, finally, pass an arduous state examination. Architects will generally charge between 10 and 16 percent of the construction cost of the project for full services. These services include preliminary design, design development, construction documents, bidding and negotiation, and construction administration. The higher percentage is for smaller projects and remodels.

House designers, on the other hand, do not have the architect's disciplinal training or formal background; many, however, are quite proficient at what they do. A house designer has frequently gained experience as an interior designer or has worked as a contractor. The fees will vary, but will likely be less than the fee of an architect.

The design fee generally reflects the amount of work and expertise that will go into your project. With any project, there are many alternatives and variables. For a higher fee, you are essentially paying for a more thorough evaluation of design options. A higher fee generally reflects more detailed drawings, more services, and fewer problems during construction.

How do you find an architect or design professional for your project? A list of candidates may come from friends, magazines, or referrals from professional societies. Many architects belong to the American Institute of Architects (A.I.A.). The A.I.A. referral list and awards programs may suggest firms to interview. Some local A.I.A. chapters maintain portfolios of members' work. For house designers, check the nearest chapter of the American Institute of Building Designers for the same information.

When you have selected several candidates, arrange an appointment with each of them. Normally, there is no charge for this initial meeting, if you meet at the design professional's office. Bring along photographs of work you like. Share as much as you can about your tastes, lifestyle, and plans for your piece of property or remodel. Ask to see the candidate's portfolio. You may also ask for the names of clients who have undertaken similar projects, ideally completed projects. Ask the owners if the design professional listened to them and applied their thoughts to the design. Was he or she easy to work with? Were cost estimates accurate? And most important, if the owners had to do it all over again, would they select the same person?

During the initial interview, discuss your proposed budget, the design professional's fees, and your timetable. Find out who will work on your project and how long it will take the design professional to complete your plans. Make sure you are comfortable with the individual you select. If you don't feel at ease, find someone else, because eventually you will need to talk about intimate matters concerning your aspirations, habits, and finances.

Be honest about your budget. If you tell an architect your budget with contingencies is "X" amount, and it's really $20,000 over that, your architect will endeavor to exclude options he or she thinks you may not be able to afford. Some of these options would likely increase the beauty and value of your project, resulting in a more satisfying home. The more common problem, however, is the opposite—thinking you can get more square footage and higher-end finish materials than your budget allows. Your architect should know prices, and if he or she says something is too costly, listen carefully. If you insist on keeping a high-end finish material, such as hardwood floors, perhaps you may need to leave one or two rooms unfinished. An important part of an architect's job is providing you with the maximum home for every dollar you spend.

Whether you work with an architect or a house designer, you will likely sign a contract or letter of agreement. A retainer is often required in advance. The rest of the payments will be based upon actual hours spent, or a percentage of completion, with the retainer credited to the final bills. You will also be required to pay certain out-of-pocket expenses incurred on your project, such as long-distance phone calls, mileage to and from the site, and blueprinting costs.

When you have made your selection, complete *The Home Design Handbook* (if you haven't already) and invite the design professional to your home, even if you are building a new home. This will be a good opportunity to communicate how you live and your likes and dislikes. Communication is the vital link to a well-tailored design.

Once the design professional has your input, he or she begins preparing schematic diagrams. When a direction has been selected (this may take several meetings), the design professional begins preliminary drawings. If you are not enthused about the design as it unfolds, stop the process until you have time to reflect on your dissatisfaction. If the design is not clear, you may request a mass model, for which there may be an additional charge. Once the design is set and the subsequent phases begin, any design changes may become an added cost to you.

When your preliminary drawings are completed, the design professional will likely provide a rough cost estimate. If the price is too high, changes will be made before proceeding into the design development phase. During the design development phase, building components will be more thoroughly defined and a revised, more accurate cost estimate given. If the revised costs and design are found acceptable, the next phase, called construction documents, begins. Construction documents are the detailed drawings and specifications from which a contractor makes a formal bid, the building department issues the building permit, and a lender can decide whether a loan will be approved. Keep listening to professional advice about the cost of building materials and detailing. As stated earlier, people often make the mistake of thinking that somehow they can build their project for less.

When the construction document phase begins, there will still be much opportunity for your input, working out all of the refinements and details. At each stage, make sure you understand the drawings. Continue to ask the design professional for probable costs and compare them to your budget. During this phase, you will visit various showrooms to select your lighting and plumbing fixtures and various finish materials such as door hardware, carpeting, flooring, paint, and wallcoverings.

When your construction documents are completed, the design professional will assist you in bidding and negotiating with a contractor, if you have contracted for full services. The design professional will ensure that each contractor is bidding on exactly the same project description. When all the bids are received, it will be tempting to select the lowest bid. However, be wary of a bid that is substantially below the others. Perhaps the contractor overlooked something major and will later request an "extra," or maybe the contractor plans to cut corners in workmanship and materials. The design professional will be able to assist you in evaluating the bids and negotiating a contract with the selected general contractor.

During the construction phase, if you have purchased construction administration services, the design professional will make site visits, write field reports, approve substitutions and requests for payments by the contractor. Also, if changes to the contract are necessary, the design professional can assist in evaluating and recommending their acceptance or modification. The design professional's continued involvement during the construction phase increases the likelihood of a successful project.

A tip: During construction, before walls are closed, take photographs or a video of electrical wiring and plumbing locations. In the future, when you need to hang a picture, repair a problem, or even remodel, you will appreciate the assurance of knowing you won't be causing undue damage.

SELECTING A CONTRACTOR

1. Investigate your builder's reputation for:

   _____ experience with similar projects

   _____ knowledge of building codes

   _____ reputation for integrity and on-budget delivery

   _____ reputation for dependability and on-time delivery

   _____ quality of workmanship

   _____ quality of products used

   _____ personality

2. What do past customers report about your builder's work? Ask how problems were resolved. How did the contractor handle a less-than-satisfactory performance from a subcontractor? Did the contractor finish the final end-of-project details satisfactorily? Did the contractor stick to his time schedule and prices? Most important, ask your references if they would hire this contractor again.

3. Ask the builder to show you a completed project, just before move-in. Ask for a range of times when you can visit a project-in-progress. If you visit a job and see everything under control—workers in action, everything reasonably tidy—that's a good sign.

4. Check with your local Better Business Bureau and the Consumer Protection Agency to see whether anyone has filed a complaint against the builder you are considering.

5. Is your builder licensed, bonded, insured, and covered by Workmen's Compensation? (If not, you could be held financially responsible for workers' injuries on your property.)

SHOULD YOU BE YOUR OWN CONTRACTOR?

Many people become excited with the possibility of saving 15 to 20 percent of the cost of construction, the builder's profit and overhead. Keep in mind that of the 15 to 20 percent profit and overhead, 10 percent of that is usually overhead, what the contractor needs to stay in business and run his crews: office, equipment, employees, insurance, taxes, and licenses. The remaining 5 to 10 percent profit is not excessive for the expertise of running a construction project well. Before venturing forth into the world of general contracting, ask yourself:

1. Are you knowledgeable about construction?
2. Are you skilled in construction?
3. Do you know qualified subcontractors?
4. Do you have the time and patience to supervise extremely complex operations?
5. Will you save more money than you could earn at your regular job?
6. Can you oversee workers?
7. Are you well organized and able to handle scheduling and volumes of paperwork?
8. Can you respond to emergencies well?

If you answered no to any of the previous questions, you will probably learn very quickly that contractors earn their money and that they are skilled professionals. However, if you are still convinced you want the job, read some of the books on doing your own contracting listed in the Annotated Bibliography. Also, be aware that in a busy market, subcontractors will give your job lower priority than repeat business from general contractors.

"Never underestimate the difficulty of orchestrating a complex job involving many people and getting each one to perform at the right time, not to mention solving technical problems in a slab while the concrete is hardening."

—Scott T. Ballard, A.I.A.,
How to Be Your Own Architect

THE BUILDING CONTRACT

Successful contracts between owners and general contractors incorporate several common elements.

THE WORK

A thorough description of the project and the duties and obligations of both parties is essential if future disagreements are to be kept at a minimum. The construction drawings, specifications, and general conditions of the contract must be clear. Your contractor should visit the site, carefully read the blueprints and specifications, and note areas that need further clarification.

Jim Locke, author of *The Well-Built House,* states: "Every sheet of paper should be dated and initialed by owner, architect, and builder. Any notes on blueprints or specs, written in after the pages are printed, should be dated and initialed. Most major problems in buildings come from lack of clarity about who said what, and when he said or drew it. The bid package combined with the contract itself become the contract documents."

THE TIME

Many contracts specify a required maximum completion time (barring unforeseen circumstances). A contract may include a daily penalty clause (called liquidated damages) for periods extending beyond the time allotted. The owner should realize that a tight time period may result in a higher contingency built into the contractor's bid. Therefore, some slack period usually works best for both parties.

THE FEE

The two most common methods of pricing are fixed-bid and cost-plus. The fixed bid usually is derived through competitive bidding among several contractors. If the scope of work is clearly described, this process may result in the lowest cost to the owner. Also, the bid amount is guaranteed by the contractor, and unless changes to the contract occur, the owner knows his exact costs. A fixed bid includes the contractor's materials, labor, allowance items (when the owner has not had time to select the actual brand or model number, such as for appliances or lighting fixtures), subcontractor bids, profit and overhead, and a contingency to cover oversights or errors. Note that allowance items are a fixed dollar amount in the contract; overruns and underruns on the allowance items are the responsibility of the client. The cost of ordering, transporting, and installing the material should be included in the contractor's bid, while the cost of the selected materials is the allowance. In a fixed bid, the contractor's books are closed to the owner and deviations between estimated and actual costs directly affect the contractor's profit. By guaranteeing the project cost, the contractor takes the risk.

A cost-plus arrangement is different because the owner becomes the risk taker. If the actual building costs are lower than the contractor's estimate, then the owner receives the benefit. (Sometimes this cost savings is shared, as an incentive to the contractor.) But if the actual building costs are higher, the owner must pay the difference. An advantage to this method is that the contractor cannot pocket an unused contingency if the project runs smoothly. Also, there are no secrets. Per contract, the owner agrees to pay a percentage above the contractor's hard costs (for profit and overhead) and the contractor's books are open to the owner, who will know the actual cost of each item. A disadvantage to this method is that efficiency is harder to assess. If the crew takes a long coffee break, you may be paying for it. Although the contractor's uncertainties have been eliminated and he can concentrate on quality, your uncertainties have increased. A cost-plus arrangement works most successfully when you trust your contractor's integrity and business practices.

CHANGE ORDERS

Change orders alter the owner/contractor agreement by changing the cost and/or completion time of the project. Perhaps you'll want to add a detail or move a window. If you plan to stay within your budget, changes will need to be kept to a minimum. When changes are desired or required, make sure you understand their effects. Unless it's an emergency, don't approve a change until you receive a written statement from the contractor stating any resulting changes in price and/or time. Accepted change orders must be signed by the owner, the contractor, and preferably the architect, too.

CLOSING OUT A PROJECT

Make sure you understand the right to lien in your state. In Washington State, we request a lien release from all suppliers and subcontractors as well as the general contractor before final payment is issued to anyone who has provided goods or services to the project. Otherwise, you may be liable to pay twice for the same item, once to the contractor and finally to the supplier. Failure on the contractor's part to pay a supplier could result in a lien being filed against your property.

When the project is nearly completed, the contractor and design professional should write a final punchlist on all the unfinished odds and ends. Most of the list may be obvious to the builder, but it should be recorded and dated anyway. If a design professional is not involved, the owner will generate the list with the contractor. Be sure to include a final cleanup of your house and site, if stated in your contract. Discuss all punchlist items with your contractor so that each person is aware of the other's expectations. Do all you can to keep your business communications open and fair. And try to find some time for fun, because building a house can be the most rewarding *and* frustrating experience you'll ever encounter. By the time you've finished, you will have intimately experienced the meaning of "bittersweet"—but more sweet than bitter, we hope, with the help of this book.

"When the punchlist and the moving in are behind you all, have a party. Human beings like ceremony, and settling their differences with food and drink. Invite everyone who worked on the project, if you are willing. There aren't many rules for such a gathering, though matters of business should be left to another occasion. It's time to step back and admire your addition to the world's landscape, and celebrate the start of your new life at home."

—Jim Locke,
The Well-Built House

TABLE 1

FIRE SPRINKLER SYSTEMS

Many fire industry experts believe that fire sprinkler systems could become standard in all new construction by 1995, just as smoke detectors are now.

A home sprinkler system consists of a network of plastic or metal pipes that runs from the main water line to the attic, where pipes are attached to ceiling joists. Quick-response sprinkler heads protrude through the ceiling or walls. The system uses the same water supply as the rest of the house, but with its own set of valves, drains, gauges, and an alarm. Installation costs for a new single-family home are approximately $1.50 per square foot. Before considering this option, determine your water pressure and flow rates to verify that they are adequate to provide for this additional system.

Standard homeowner's insurance should cover any damage due to the sprinklers, but check with your insurance agent before the installation. Also, ask if you might qualify for reduced fire insurance rates.

STANDARD 13D:
LIMITED AREA, LIMITED COST

The National Fire Protection Association's (NFPA) Standard 13D, which details the installation of sprinkler systems in one- and two-family dwellings and mobile homes, allows the omission of sprinkler heads from areas in the home where fire is less likely to occur. Omitted areas include:

- bathrooms measuring less than 55 square feet and equipped with noncombustible fixtures;
- closets measuring less than 24 square feet that have walls and ceilings surfaced with noncombustible materials;
- garages, open attached porches, carports, and similar structures;
- attics, crawl spaces, and other concealed areas not intended for living or storage purposes; and
- entrance foyers that are not the only means of egress.

Designed to 13D specs, the sprinkler system will cover 70 to 80 percent of the home, and about 86 percent of those areas where fatal fires originate. Such variances translate into less pipe, fewer fittings, and reduced labor, all of which may bring the cost of residential fire sprinklers down to an affordable level.

NFPA's 13D is not mandated, but is a voluntary standard that guides installers on the design and placement of residential sprinkler systems. For more information, contact NFPA at (617) 770-3000.

TABLE 2

ENERGY CONSERVATION MEASURES

1. Caulk sill plates and any connections during exterior wall framing and finishing.
2. Use foam-type caulking at vent stacks and other roof, wall, and floor penetrations.
3. Apply a vapor barrier to the warm-side surface of exterior walls and ceiling framing.
4. In heating climates, you may wish to add an exterior air-infiltration barrier. Make sure this material is water permeable so that moisture is not trapped in exterior walls.
5. Caulk and weatherstrip around windows, doors, and thresholds.
6. Insulate hot water lines and forced-air ducts.
7. Insulate bathtubs and spas.
8. Before purchasing windows, check their rating for air infiltration.
9. Make sure exhaust vents are dampered.
10. Install a rain cap on the chimney and a flue damper above the firebox. Make sure the fire damper is tight when closed.
11. Install adequate roof venting to prevent moisture in the attic and/or rafters.

12. For an unheated attic, install insulation (with a vapor barrier) between the floor joists.
13. Provide door and window protection from winter winds with garden walls or evergreen landscaping.
14. Cut water consumption in half by installing high-performance low-flow faucet aerators and shower heads, and use a water-conserving dishwasher and clothes washer.
15. Set water heater temperature between 110 and 120 degrees Fahrenheit.
16. Install shading devices or deciduous landscaping for protection of south-facing windows.
17. Install double-glazed windows with Low-E (Low Emittance) Glass.
18. Consult your local building department, utility company, or state energy extension service (Table 3) for thermal insulation recommendations.

TABLE 3
STATE ENERGY EXTENSION SERVICE CONTACTS

The national Energy Extension Service (EES) is a federal/state partnership authorized by Congress to give personalized information and technical assistance to small-scale energy users on energy conservation and the use of renewable and abundant resources. Every state and territory receives grants to work closely with families, owners of small companies, and local government officials to help them take practical steps to conserve energy.

ALABAMA
Energy Extension Service
Division of Science and Technology
3465 Norman Bridge Road
Montgomery, Alabama 36105
(205) 284-8936

ALASKA
Rural Development Division
949 East 36th Avenue,
Suite 400
Anchorage, Alaska 99508
(907) 563-1955

AMERICAN SAMOA
Territorial Energy Office
Office of the Governor
Pago Pago, American Samoa 96799
(684) 699-1325

ARIZONA
Energy Office
Arizona Department of Commerce
1700 West Washington, 5th Floor
Phoenix, Arizona 85007
(602) 255-3632

ARKANSAS
Energy Programs
Arkansas Energy Office
No. 1 State Capitol Mall
Little Rock, Arkansas 72201
(501) 371-1370

CALIFORNIA
California Energy Extension Service
Governor's Office of Planning and
Research
1400 Tenth Street
Sacramento, California 95814
(916) 323-4388

COLORADO
Colorado Energy Extension Service
Colorado Office of Energy Conservation
112 East 14th Avenue
Denver, Colorado 80203
(303) 894-2144

CONNECTICUT
Office of Policy and Management
Energy Division
80 Washington Street
Hartford, Connecticut 06106
(203) 566-2800

DELAWARE
Division of Facilities Management
Energy Office
P.O. Box 1401, O'Neill Building
Federal Street
Dover, Delaware 19903
(800) 282-8616 (Delaware only)
(302) 736-5644

DISTRICT OF COLUMBIA
DC Energy Office
613 G Street, N.W., Room 500
Washington, DC 20004
(202) 727-1800

FLORIDA
Governor's Energy Office
214 South Brounough
Tallahassee, Florida 32301
(904) 488-2475

GEORGIA
Office of Energy Resources
270 Washington Street, S.W.,
Room 615
Atlanta, Georgia 30334
(404) 656-5176

GUAM
Guam Energy Office
P.O. Box 2950
Agana, Guam 96910
(671) 734-4452/4530 (overseas
operator)

HAWAII
Department of Planning and Economic Development
P.O. Box 2359
Honolulu, Hawaii 96804
(808) 548-3033

IDAHO
Energy Division of the Idaho Department of Water Resources
State House Mail
Boise, Idaho 83720
1-800-334-SAVE

ILLINOIS
Consumer Assistance and Residential Conservation Service
Department of Energy and Natural Resources
325 West Adams, Room 300
Springfield, Illinois 62704
(217) 785-2800

INDIANA
Energy Extension Service
Indiana Commerce Center
One North Capitol
Indianapolis, Indiana 46204-2288
(317) 232-8995

IOWA
Energy Bureau
Division of Energy and Geological Resources
Iowa Department of Natural Resources
Wallace State Office Building
Des Moines, Iowa 50319
(515) 281-5145

KANSAS
Energy Extension Service
Kansas State University
Ward Hall
Manhattan, Kansas 66506
(913) 532-6026

KENTUCKY
Division of Conservation
Kentucky Energy Cabinet
P.O. Box 11888
Lexington, Kentucky 40578-1916
(606) 252-5535

LOUISIANA
Energy Extension Service Program
Energy Division
Department of Natural Resources
P.O. Box 44156
Baton Rouge, Louisiana 70804-4156
(504) 342-2133

MAINE
Energy Extension Service
Maine Office of Energy Resources
State House, Station No. 53
Augusta, Maine 04333
(207) 289-3811

MARYLAND
Department of Housing and Community Development
45 Calvert Street
Annapolis, Maryland 21401
(301) 974-3751

MASSACHUSETTS
Residential Division
Executive Office of Energy Resources
100 Cambridge Street, Room 1103
Boston, Massachusetts 02202
(617) 727-4732

MICHIGAN
Energy Programs
Michigan Department of Commerce
6545 Mercantile Way
P.O. Box 30221
Lansing, Michigan 48909
(517) 334-6264

MINNESOTA
Information and Technical Assistance
Energy Division
Department of Public Service
900 American Center Building
150 East Kellogg Boulevard
St. Paul, Minnesota 55101
(612) 297-1965

MISSISSIPPI
Coordinator, Energy Extension Service Program
Mississippi State University
Box 5446

Starkville, Mississippi 39762
(601) 325-3152

MISSOURI
Department of Natural Resources
Division of Energy
Community Assistance Programs
P.O. Box 176
Jefferson City, Missouri 65102
(314) 751-4000

MONTANA
Conservation and Renewable Energy Bureau
Energy Division
Department of Natural Resources and Conservation
1520 East 6th Avenue
Helena, Montana 59620-2301
(406) 444-6697

NEBRASKA
SECP/EES Program Manager
Nebraska State Energy Office
P.O. Box 95085, 9th Floor
State Capitol Building
Lincoln, Nebraska 68509
(402) 471-2867

NEVADA
Energy Program Manager
Office of Community Services
1100 East Williams, Suite 117
Carson City, Nevada 89710
(702) 885-4420

NEW HAMPSHIRE
Energy Extension Services
Governor's Energy Office
2½ Beacon Street, 2nd Floor
Concord, New Hampshire 03301
(603) 271-2711

NEW JERSEY
Community and Educational Services
New Jersey Department of Commerce and Economic Development,
Energy Division
101 Commerce Street
Newark, New Jersey 07102
(800) 492-4242 (New Jersey only)
(201) 648-3185

NEW MEXICO
Building & Demonstration Program
Bureau
New Mexico Energy, Minerals &
Natural Gas Development
525 Camino de los Marquez
Santa Fe, New Mexico 87501
(505) 827-5882

NEW YORK
Director of Communications
New York State Energy Office
2 Rockefeller Plaza, 10th Floor
Albany, New York 12223
(800) 342-3722 (New York only)
(518) 473-4375

NORTH CAROLINA
North Carolina Department of
Commerce
Energy Division
430 N. Salisbury Street
Raleigh, North Carolina 27611
(919) 733-2230

NORTH DAKOTA
Office of Intergovernmental Assistance
State Capitol, 14th Floor
Bismarck, North Dakota 58505
(701) 224-2094

NORTHERN MARIANA ISLANDS
Office of Energy
P.O. Box 340
Saipan, Mariana Islands 96950
(670) 322-9229
(670) 322-9236

OHIO
Department of Development
Community Development Division
Office of Energy Conservation
30 East Broad Street, 24th Floor
Columbus, Ohio 43266-0413
(614) 466-6797

OKLAHOMA
Energy Information Center
Oklahoma Department of Commerce
6601 Broadway
Oklahoma City, Oklahoma 73116
(800) 522-8573 (Oklahoma only)
(405) 521-3941

OREGON
Energy Extension Leader
OSU Extension Energy Program
344 Batcheller
Oregon State University
Corvallis, Oregon 97331-2401
(503) 754-3004

PENNSYLVANIA
Administration
Pennsylvania Energy Office
116 Pine Street
Harrisburg, Pennsylvania 17105
(717) 783-0225

PUERTO RICO
Conservation Program
Office of Energy
Office of the Governor
P.O. Box 41089-Minillas Station
Santurce, Puerto Rico 00940-1089
(809) 721-4570

RHODE ISLAND
Governor's Office of Energy Assistance
275 Westminster Mall
Providence, Rhode Island 02903
(401) 277-3370/6920

SOUTH CAROLINA
State Energy Office
1205 Pendelton Street, 3rd Floor
Columbia, South Carolina 29211
(803) 734-1740

SOUTH DAKOTA
Energy Extension Service
Energy Office
217½ West Missouri
Pierre, South Dakota 57501-4516
(605) 773-3603

TENNESSEE
Energy Division
Department of Economic and Community Development
320 6th Avenue North, 6th Floor
Nashville, Tennessee 37219-5308
(615) 741-6671

TEXAS
Energy Efficiency Division
Public Utility Commission
7800 Shoal Creek Boulevard
Suite 400 North
Austin, Texas 78757
(512) 458-0301

TRUST TERRITORY OF THE PACIFIC ISLANDS
Office of Capital Improvement Programs
Trust Territory of the Pacific Islands
Saipan, Mariana Islands 96950
(670) 322-9333

UTAH
Energy Extension Service
Utah Energy Office
3 Triad Center, Suite 450

Salt Lake City, Utah 84180-1204
(800) 662-3633 (Utah only)
(801) 538-5428

VERMONT
Energy Program Coordinator
Cooperative Extension Service
VO-TECH Department
Agricultural Engineering Building
University of Vermont
Burlington, Vermont 05405
(802) 656-2001

VIRGIN ISLANDS
Virgin Islands Energy Office
P.O. Box 2996
St. Thomas, Virgin Islands 00801
(809) 774-6726

Development Engineer
Old Customs House
Fredericksted
St. Croix, Virgin Islands 00840
(809) 772-2616

VIRGINIA
Division of Energy
Department of Mines, Minerals, and
Energy
2201 West Broad Street
Richmond, Virginia 23220
(800) 552-3831 (Virginia only)
(804) 367-6851

WASHINGTON
Energy Extension Service
Washington State Energy Office
809 Legion Way, S.E., Mail Stop
FA-11
Olympia, Washington 98504
(206) 586-5089

WEST VIRGINIA
EES Coordinator
West Virginia Fuel and Energy
Division
Governor's Office of Community
and Industrial Development
1204 Kanawaha Boulevard East
Charleston, West Virginia 25301
(304) 348-8860

WISCONSIN
Program Operations
Wisconsin Division of State Energy
Department of Administration
South Webster, 6th Floor
P.O. Box 7868
Madison, Wisconsin 53707
(608) 266-6850

WYOMING
Wyoming Energy Extension Service
Werner Tech Building, Casper
College
125 College Drive
Casper, Wyoming 82601
(307) 266-4904

TABLE 4

NATIONAL SOLAR ORGANIZATIONS

These organizations can provide information about solar energy or other renewable sources.

Conservation and Renewable Energy
Inquiry and Referral Service
(CAREIRS)
P.O. Box 8900
Silver Spring, Maryland 29007
(800) 523-2929

Florida State Energy Center
3000 State Road 401
Cape Canaveral, Florida 32920
(407) 783-0300

National Appropriate Technology
Assistance Service (NATAS)
P.O. Box 2525
Butte, Montana 59702-2525
(800) 428-2525

National Center for Appropriate
Technology
P.O. Box 3838
Butte, Montana 59702
(406) 494-4577

Oak Ridge National Laboratory
P.O. Box 2008
Oak Ridge, Tennessee 37831-6070
(615) 574-4346
(provides an insulation fact sheet)

Solar Energy Research Institute
(SERI)
1536 Cole Boulevard
Golden, Colorado 80401
(303) 231-1192

TABLE 5

LIGHTING PRINCIPLES

1. Buy compact fluorescent bulbs. A single 18-watt compact fluorescent lamp produces the same light as a 75-watt incandescent lamp and lasts thirteen

times as long. Incredibly, this single lamp will add one ton less of carbon dioxide and twenty pounds less of sulfur dioxide to the atmosphere than does the equivalent incandescent bulb. These fluorescents emit naturally colored light and don't flicker or hum. Their only drawback is they are expensive to use with a dimmer. To blend fluorescent lighting with incandescent lamps, use one of the following:

— most low-wattage PL (5- to 13-watt) fluorescent fixtures
— MR-16 with color-correcting filters
— fluorescent lamps with color temperatures of approximately 2,700 to 3,000 degrees Kelvin (K).

2. If you want your indoor lighting to be as close to sunlight as possible, consider "full-spectrum" fluorescent tubes that simulate sunlight.
3. For reading light, consider Chromalux full-spectrum bulbs. They intensify colors and sharpen black-and-white contrasts, making reading easier on the eyes.
4. To save energy, put the light where it is needed rather than flooding areas with light. Install dimmers on overhead lights and make sure task lighting can be individually controlled. Follow these guidelines:

    Ambient, or general, light illumines the interior with a soft level of light and makes one aware of the shape and dimensions of a space.

    Task light is the light by which you read, cook, and sew; it allows you to see book titles or stereo knobs.

    Accent light is decorative, usually built-in concealed light that directs attention to artwork or architectural features.
5. Study the effects of natural daylight on a natural landscape to understand lighting modulations from hard to soft and how light reacts when filtered or directed.
6. Light the walls, not the floors. In general, minimize overhead lights centered in the ceiling that cast their glow on the floor. Walls are what are noticed when we enter a room, and walls are likely to have more items of visual interest than the floors.
7. Windows become black mirrors at night. To see beyond windows when it is dark, provide dimmers on selected interior lights. The dimmer the inside lighting level, the more can be seen outside the window.

TABLE 6

LIGHTING REFERENCE TABLE

HOW MUCH LIGHT?

The amount of light needed depends on the size of the room and the types of fixtures. Here are some guidelines from the American Lighting Association.

The actual light from a fixture depends on how the light source is shielded and the type of bulb.

Area	Pendants and Ceiling Lights	Recessed Fixtures	Wall Lights
Small room, under 150 sq. ft.	Three to five incandescent lamps for a total of 100–150 watts, or 35–60 fluorescent watts.	Four 75-watt incandescent lamps, or 80 fluorescent watts.	Four 50-watt reflector lamps or 60–80 fluorescent watts.
Medium room, 150–250 sq. ft.	Four to six incandescent lamps for a total of 200–300 watts, or 60–80 fluorescent watts.	Four 100-watt incandescent lamps, or 120 fluorescent watts.	Five to eight 75-watt incandescent reflector lamps, or 120–160 fluorescent watts.
Large room, over 250 sq. ft.	One incandescent lamp per 125 sq. ft. for a total of 1 watt per sq. ft., or 1/3 fluorescent watt per sq. ft.	100–150 incandescent watts per 50 sq. ft., or 160–200 fluorescent watts.	One 75-watt incandescent reflector lamp per 25 sq. ft., or 160 fluorescent watts.

For professional advice on lighting your home, call the toll-free number: 1-800-BRIGHT-IDEAS.

ANNOTATED
BIBLIOGRAPHY

Ajay, Betty. *Betty Ajay's Guide to Home Landscaping*. New York: McGraw-Hill
Book Company, 1970.
*Older yet relevant book on practical ideas for home landscaping. Read the chapter on
terrace placement.*

Alexander, Christopher, Sara Ishikawa, and Murray Silverstein. *A Pattern Language*. New York: Oxford University Press, 1977.
*This valuable and well-researched book offers interesting psychological explanations as to
why certain design patterns feel comfortable and others do not.*

Anderson, Bruce, and Malcolm Wells. *Passive Solar Energy: The Homeowners Guide
to Natural Heating and Cooling*. Andover, Mass.: Brick House Publishing Company, 1981.
A basic, easy-to-understand book on passive solar energy.

Baker, John Milnes. *How to Build a House with an Architect*. New York: Harper
and Row, 1988.

Written by an architect, this book is useful to anyone who will be working with an architect for a home design or remodeling an existing house. The author describes how to work most effectively with an architect throughout the design and construction process, what kinds of decisions to make, and how to avoid cost overruns.

Ballard, Scott T. *How to Be Your Own Architect.* White Hall, Va.: Betterway Publications, Inc., 1987.
Read the sections on practical design, aesthetic design, and details.

Better Homes and Gardens. *Adding On.* Des Moines, Iowa: Meredith Corporation, 1984.
A perfect book for those embarking on home remodeling projects; from the All About Your House series.

————. *Garages, Basements, & Attics.* Des Moines, Iowa: Meredith Corporation, 1985.
If you want to remodel your garage, basement, or attic, this is the book for you.

————. *Solar Living.* Des Moines, Iowa: Meredith Corporation, 1983.
A practical and well-photographed book on residential solar options from the All About Your House series.

Boericke, Art, and Barry Shapiro. *Handmade Houses.* San Francisco, Calif.: The Scrimshaw Press, 1973.
A lovely photographic account of "lay" architecture.

Ching, Francis D. K., and Dale E. Miller. *Home Renovation.* New York: Van Nostrand Reinhold, 1983.
A thorough and practical book, written by an architect, about planning and design considerations of home remodeling; describes construction methods and illustrates details.

Coen, Patricia, and Bryan Milford. *Closets: Designing and Organizing the Personalized Closet.* New York: Grove Weidenfeld, 1988.
Step-by-step approach to creating well-organized, fully utilized closets. Extensive color photographs and illustrations.

Conran, Terence. *The Bed and Bath Book*. New York: Crown Publishers, 1978.
Excellent photographic reference covering all bed and bath considerations.

———. *The Kitchen Book*. New York: Crown Publishers, 1977.
A beautifully photographed reference book that will help the reader with layout and storage considerations, lighting, and work surface materials.

———. *New House Book*. New York: Crown Publishers, 1985.
An excellent photographic reference and idea book. Mr. Conran's introduction, "A Taste for Simplicity," is a "must read."

Dadd, Debra Lynn. *The Nontoxic Home*. Los Angeles: J. P. Tarcher, 1986.
A basic guide for creating a nontoxic home.

DiDonno, Lupe, and Phyllis Sperling. *How to Design and Build Your Own Home*. New York: Alfred A. Knopf, 1978.
Chapter 1, "Functional Space Planning," allows the reader to consider various functional relationships within the home.

Fell, Derek. *The Complete Garden Planning Manual*. Los Angeles: HP Books, 1989.
Compiled by a team of gardening experts, this encyclopedic volume takes the reader through the evaluation and decision-making process; richly photographed.

Gault, Lila, and Jeffrey Weiss. *Small Houses*. New York: Warner Books, Inc., 1980.
A delightfully photographed account of carefully detailed homes of less than 1,200 square feet.

Goldbeck, David. *The Smart Kitchen*. Woodstock, New York: Ceres Press, 1989.
Ideas for creating an ecologically responsive kitchen. Good information on pros and cons of flooring and countertop materials.

Good, Clint, and Debra Lynn Dadd. *Healthful Houses: How to Design and Build Your Own*. Bethesda, Maryland: Guaranty Press, 1988.

Written by an architect and a consumer advocate, this practical book is for health-minded individuals. Architects and builders will appreciate recommended products and specifications arranged according to the industry standard outlined by the Construction Specifications Institute.

Halacy, Dan. *Home Energy: Your Best Options for Solar Heating and Cooling, Wood, Wind, and Photovoltaics.* Emmaus, Pa.: Rodale Press, 1984.
An excellent reference for residential energy options.

Ireys, Alice. *Garden Designs.* New York: Prentice-Hall, 1991.
Flower garden design ideas from Prentice-Hall's American Gardening series.

Jacobsen, Max, et al. *The Good House: Contrast as a Design Tool.* Newtown, Conn.: The Taunton Press, Inc., 1990.
Written in nontechnical language, the architect-authors explain how homes can be designed to be satisfying in deeper ways—aesthetically, emotionally, intellectually, and spiritually.

Kira, Alexander. *The Bathroom.* New York: Viking Press, 1976.
Written by a Cornell University professor who has spent over twenty years studying all aspects of the bathroom.

Lamb, Curt. *Homestyles.* New York: St. Martin's Press, 1979.
This book contains awareness activities that build feelings into your home.

Langdon, Philip. *American Houses.* New York: Stewart, Tabori, & Chang, 1987.
Well-written and well-researched book on home design ideas with more than 200 color photographs and illustrations. Excellent section on home energy.

Lester, Kent, and Dave McGuerty. *The Complete Guide to Contracting Your Home.* White Hall, Va.: Betterway Publications, Inc., 1986.
Subtitled "A Step-by-Step Method for Managing Home Construction," this 279-page book is comprehensive. Each of the twenty-seven chapters in the Project Management section covers a basic trade such as drywall or electrical. The book includes a glossary of construction terms and many reproducible forms and contracts.

Locke, Jim. *The Well-Built House*. Boston, Mass.: Houghton Mifflin Company, 1988.
Essential reading for working with a general contractor. Good sections on pros and cons of various building materials. The author, a builder and one of the heroes of Tracy Kidder's House, *writes in a friendly and informative style.*

McGrath, Molly, and Norman McGrath. *Children's Spaces: 50 Architects & Designers Create Environments for the Young*. New York: William Morrow & Company, Inc., 1978.
Architects and designers share their design ideas for children's rooms.

Nisson, J. D., and Gautum Dutt. *The Superinsulated Home Book*. New York: John Wiley & Sons, Inc., 1985.
A basic guide on the design and construction of superinsulated homes.

Pearson, David. *The Natural House Book*. New York: Simon & Schuster, 1989.
Thorough how-tos on creating a healthy, harmonious, and ecologically sound home environment. Beautifully photographed and illustrated.

Rauch, Paul H. *How to Be Your Own Contractor*. Andover, Mass.: Brick House Publishing Company, 1988.
Subtitled "Remodeling, Additions, Alterations, Building a New Home," this 102-page manual covers lot selection, financing, house plan preparation, cost estimating, and construction schedules.

Rose, Graham. *The Small Garden Planner*. New York: Simon & Schuster, 1987.
Excellent source book for improving or creating a small garden to suit various climate, site, style, and budget considerations; 200 color photographs and 60 design plans.

Roskind, Robert. *Before You Build*. Berkeley, Calif.: Ten Speed Press, 1983.
A good reference book and workbook covering such topics as buying land, solar heating, water and waste systems, permits, codes and inspections, financing, and estimating.

Schmidt, Kathryn. *The Home Remodeling Management Book*. Palo Alto, Calif.: Egger Publications, 1987.

Written by an architect, this 188-page book is well organized and easy to use. The workbook format emphasizes tracking costs and progress and staying on top of project management.

Schoen, Elin. *The Closet Book.* New York: Harmony Books, 1982.
An excellent book for storage ideas; abundant color photographs.

Scutella, Richard M., and David Heberle. *How to Plan, Contract and Build Your Own Home.* Blue Ridge Summit, Pa.: TAB Books, Inc., 1987.
Practical advice on general contracting duties.

Sexton, Richard. *The Cottage Book.* San Francisco, Calif.: Chronicle Books, 1989.
Beautifully photographed and inspiring book about small-scale projects.

Sheehan, Philip B., ed. *The McGraw-Hill Home Book.* New York: McGraw-Hill, Inc., 1980.
An analytical approach for home remodeling projects.

Strong, Steven. *The Solar Electric House: A Design Manual for Home-Scale Photovoltaic Power Systems.* Emmaus, Pa.: Rodale Press, 1986.
A useful reference manual for those in remote areas beyond the reach of power lines.

Sunset Books. *Home Lighting Handbook.* Menlo Park, Calif.: Lane Publishing Company, 1988.
Room-by-room lighting ideas for the interior and exterior of your home. Good section on the basics of lighting with photographic examples.

Szenasy, Susan. *The Home: Exciting New Designs for Today's Lifestyles.* Philadelphia, Pa.: Running Press, 1989.
A beautifully photographed and practical look at design ideas.

Torrice, Antonio F., and Ro Logrippo. *In My Room: Designing for and with Children.* New York: Fawcett Columbine, 1989.

Coauthored by Torrice, a designer and early-childhood specialist, and Logrippo, a design writer, this full-color book depicts and explains many excellent ideas for designing congenial, comfortable, and practical environments for children, from toddlers to teenagers. The authors offer techniques for eliciting and incorporating your own children's ideas in the design of their rooms.

Yepsen, Roger. "A Home for Life." In *Practical Homeowner*, July/August 1987.
This article contains many excellent ideas for designing homes that won't need to be modified as one ages.

Wacker, David Alan. *The Complete Guide to Home Security*. White Hall, Va.: Betterway Publications, Inc., 1990.
Highly recommended; written by a law enforcement professional who has gathered valuable information on making an informed assessment of one's home protection needs.

Wilson, Alex. *Consumer Guide to Home Energy Savings*. Washington, D.C.: American Council for an Energy Efficient Economy (ACEEE), 1990.
This valuable 252-page book describes energy-saving products and ranks the efficiency of furnaces, air conditioners, and all major appliances. It can be purchased for $6.95 through ACEEE, 1001 Connecticut Ave., N.W., Suite 535, Washington, D.C. 20036.

CREDITS

PICTURE CREDITS